Mama Sita's®

Fourth Generation

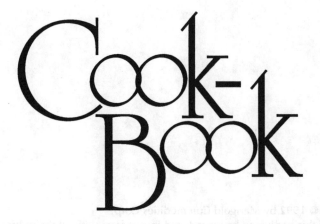

Engracia Cruz Reyes Centennial Edition

Cover design and Illustrations by:
Jong Vinoya and
Stella Duque

Printed by:
Vera-Reyes, Inc.

FOUR GENERATIONS OF FILIPINO COOKING
1892 - 1992

There are four generations of women in this "Mama Sita" book, thus the title.

The woman-seed of this lineage is Engracia Cruz-Reyes, wife to Justice Alex A. Reyes; mother to Mama Sita. Her lifestory is about a Filipina housewife who extolled and doted on Filipino cuisine. In her everyday role as a mother to a brood of thirteen she tended a happy home and a good table for her family, not of luxury as that of a Doña, but of someone who found joy in making the best out of what she had. And it was not much, in the beginning. She, like other mothers in her time had her fill of challenges in life. But Aling Asiang, as she preferred to be called, managed. How she managed family life - in simple yet inspiring ways. Where she managed - most of the time, in the "comedor", which was her little kingdom.

The grand old lady saw to it that all who shared her table would enjoy her cooking, especially because Filipino specialties were laid out. In her culinary life, she perfected her recipes, shared them with her household, served them to family and friends and later on to customers of Lapu-lapu, a student canteen adjacent to St. Theresa's College in San Marcelino. A restaurant-on-wheels followed suit, parked on Luneta every afternoon with delightful merienda fare. Shortly after her success in the food business, she prospered further and began the Aristocrat Restaurant at Dewey Boulevard (now Roxas Blvd.) The rest is culinary history.

1992 is her centennial year - Engracia Cruz-Reyes is being honored by her country as an eminent Filipina, considered an exponent of Filipino food, who put our cuisine above the rest. Aling Asiang was a nationalist and she expressed it best with her sandok and palayok. She continues to inspire us - to make the best of what we have, to think the best of and keep the faith of Filipino cuisine.

Mama Sita or Teresita Reyes-Reyes is the eldest daughter of Engracia Cruz-Reyes. As such, it was she who first experienced cooking in the "comedor" - as a dutiful daughter who helped prepare the family meals, and as a student of her mother's cooking style. She was taught how to cook the sauteeing mixture by batches so that food orders would be served faster. Their pre-preparation concept was lifted out of homegrown experience, not fastfood operations manuals.

Travel was one privilege that Mama Sita always afforded herself for in new places she learned new things, how differently people eat, the ingredients and cooking styles in situ. It was during one of her tours to the United States where she was dismayed by the manner in which Filipino food was being prepared, unfaithful to its real tastes and appearances. Her "kababayans" had forgotten what sinigang is supposed to taste like - shortcuts in cooking were a necessary evil of the hectic pace of life. Thus, poor substitutes like lemon juice sufficed as souring agent which, of course, produced a "PALEFACE" sinigang.

The idea of the instant seasonings and preparations came into being, inspired by the dilemma for her "kababayans". How to help them cook a decent "sinigang" despite the stress of work. So, she kept experimenting, cooking green sampalok, mashing, preserving, and using her formula for the "instant" sour soup. Mama Sita never stopped discussing her project with the family and friends, learning as well as giving out secrets in the process. Until one of her daughters, Clara, got keen on the matter. With husband, Dr. Bartolome Lapus, Clara was bent on producing a commercial instant sinigang that would be marketable, exportable and remain very Filipino. Thus, the beginning of a successful culinary venture, Mama Sita's Sauces & Mixes.

The fourth daughter of Mama Sita graduated with an Architectural degree, Clarita still has her school day charm, her looks are not characteristic of the Navotas Reyes genes but more of her father's, Fidel Reyes of Malolos. She is soft-spoken and unassuming unless provoked by policies that prevent Filipinos from producing and exporting more Philippine food products.

They started it all - this business of compacting the intricacies of Filipino cooking into a convenient, instant package that retains the real flavours of Filipino tastes. The sampalok used to sour sinigang, are dried, powdered and packaged. The achuete color, they extracted and powdered. They dried and literally "pulverized" the freshest natural ingredients to deliver to consumers the convenience of Caldereta, Pancit Palabok, Adobo, Kare-kare and many more. And look at how many food processing plants, even multinational companies have followed suit.

Inspite of their academic backgrounds (Dr. Lapus is a Biologist), they pioneered a food product which has boosted the industry locally and more so internationally. And there are the new products to be launched because the energetic couple have not stopped dreaming.

Last but not the least is Joyce Clarissa Reyes Lapus, of the fourth generation. The only daughter of Clara and Bart was trained to handle the products at a very tender age. Industry has no barriers in time. Pride of hard work was instilled in Joyce as early as when she was eight, her exposure to the culinary life of the three generations ahead became her vehicle for being a real cook in her own right.

This granddaughter of Mama Sita began her career in Mama Sita's Sauces & Mixes as a cooking demonstrator of their products. She was sent to all corners of the world to show to the international market how simple and healthy it is to use instant mixes free from harmful chemicals. With her youthfulness and cooking skills, she was the best passport her parents' company could have. With the encouragement they showered on their daughter, she has emerged as a culinary ambassador of goodwill. Joyce is a lively woman-child who can charm wide audiences of different venues and nationalities.

Many of the recipes in this book are hers. Some she collected from Mama Sita's Sauces and Mixes' consumers who have become friends. Most of the recipes she knows by heart and has tested hundreds of times together with cousin Vicky Rose Reyes Pacheco, chef of Chateau 1771 Restaurant. Joyce can attest that they are all practical and they render delicious results.

So there you have it, Engracia Cruz-Reyes, Mama Sita, Clara Reyes-Lapus, and Joyce. Four generations of women who have discovered the boundless joys of cooking and kept the faith of Filipino food. This book is the timeless contribution of Mama Sita, Clara and Joyce to the woman who continues to inspire them.

Nancy T. Reyes
Third Generation Reyes
Food Writer

CONTENTS

VEGETABLES

Vegetable Soup   1
Adobong Kangkong   1
Arroz Ala Mama Sita   2
Kangkong with Oyster Sauce   3
Vegetables Unlimited   3
Chopsuey   4
Pancit Buko with Oyster Sauce   5
Pinakbet (Tropical Vegetable Stew)   6
Spicy Sitaw   7
Lumpiang Gulay (Vegetable Rolls)   8
Creamy Adobo Dip   9
Stir Fried Vegetables with Garlic Sauce   10
Pancit Bihon Guisado
(Stir Fried Vegetable over Rice Noodles)   11
Ginisang Togue (Sauteed Bean Sprouts)   12
Ukoy (Shrimp Vegetable Fritters)   13
Sotanghon Bihon Guisado   14
(Stir-Fried Noodles)
Mama Sita's Lettuce Salad   15
Fried Rice with Oyster Sauce   16
Pechay Flowers (best in November)   17
Ginisang Munggo (Sauteed Mung Beans)   18
Fried Bean Curd with Oyster Sauce   19

SEAFOOD

Tom Yum Goong   21
Sinigang na Hipon   22
Seafood Chowder   23
Tuna Empanada   24
Paella Pilipina   26
Saucy Clams   28
Sweet and Sour Fish   28
Rellenong Bangus   29
Stuffed Squid   30

32 Adobong Pusit (Squid Adobo)

33 Garlic Squid

33 Spicy Sizzling Shrimps

34 Tocino'ng Isda

34 Pinangat sa Gata
(Fish Poached in Coconut Sauce)

35 Crab Lumpia (Crab Rolls)

36 Calamares (Squid Rings)

37 Steamed Lapu-Lapu

38 Hakaw

40 Easy Shrimps

40 Guinataang Hipon
(Shrimps in Coconut Sauce)

41 Special Pancit Palabok
(Noodles with Shrimps Gravy)

42 Baked Tahong (Spicy Baked Mussels)

CHICKEN

43 Sotanghon Soup

44 Sinampalukang Manok
(Tamarind Flavoured Chicken Soup)

45 Chicken Lollipop

46 Chicken Curry

47 Chicken Liver with Mixed Vegetables

48 Chicken Twist

49 Fried Chicken with Ginger Sauce

50 Pastel Del Pollo
(Stewed Chicken with Pastry Crust)

52 Diced Chicken with Cashew Nuts

53 Adobo in Coco Sauce

53 Chicken Afritada (Chicken Stewed
with Potatoes and Bell Peppers)

54 Caldereta (Spicy Stew)

MEAT

55 Almondigas

56 Wonton Soup

Beef Sinigang   57

Siopao Asado   58

Sweet and Sour Pork   60

Naiiba'ng Lumpia
(Vietnamese Spring Rolls)   61

Beef or Pork with Spinach   62

Pork Asado   62

Pinsec Frito (Crispy Wontons)   63

Baked Spare Ribs   64

Tocino (Sweet Pork)   64

Dinuguan (Blood Stew)   65

Bola Bola Con Salsa Agrio-Dulce   66
(Meat balls with Sweet and Sour Sauce)

Lumpiang Shanghai (Spring Rolls)   67

Lechon Kawali (Crispy Pork)   68

Paksiw na Lechon   69
(Pork Stew in Tangy Liver Sauce)

Barbecue   70

Paksiw na Pata (Pickled-in Pork Hocks)   70

Beef with Snow Peas   71

Kare Kare   72
(Oxtail Stewed In A Rich Peanut Sauce)

Beef with Oyster Sauce   73

Callos   74

Chili Con Carne   75

Meat Balls in White Sauce   76

Meatloaf   77

Mechado   78

Stuffed Mushroom with Oyster Sauce   79

Longganisa (Breakfast Sausage)   79

Index   81

Retail Outlets in Key Cities Worldwide   85

Vegetables

VEGETABLES SOUP

			Metric		English	
8	cups	Pork stock (from 2 Kg. boiled pork)	1.5	li.	2	quarts
1/2	tsp.	Blackpepper	1/2	tsp.	1/2	tsp..
100	g.	Pork liver, sliced	100	g.	3 1/2	oz.
1/4	cup	Mama Sita's Oyster Sauce	60	mL.	2	fl.oz.
160	g.	Carrots, sliced thinly	160	g.	5 2/3	oz.
100	g.	Pechay baguio (Chinese cabbage), sliced	100	g.	3 1/2	oz.

1. Boil the pork stock and add the blackpepper, pork liver and Oyster Sauce.

2. When the pork liver is cooked, add the carrots. Cook for another 2 minutes.

3. Add the pechay Baguio. Serve hot.

The pork stock mentioned here could be as simple as the stock you get from boiling the pork for "Lechon Kawali" and "Spare Ribs."

ADOBONG KANGKONG

			Metric		English	
2	cloves	Garlic, crushed	5	g.	1	tsp.
1	Tbsp.	Cooking oil	15	mL.	1	Tbsp.
4	Tbsp.	Mama Sita's Barbecue Marinade	60	mL.	4	Tbsps.
3	tali	Kangkong or spinach	1/4	Kg.	9	oz.
1	Tbsp.	Vinegar	15	mL.	1	Tbsp.
		Salt to taste				

1. Sauté garlic in cooking oil until golden brown.

2. Add Mama Sita's Barbecue Marinade and kangkong leaves.

3. When the leaves turn dark green, add vinegar and salt to taste.

4 Remove from heat and serve over hot rice.

ARROZ ALA MAMA SITA

Makes 4 servings.

			Metric		English	
1/2	cup	Bulaklak ng saging (banana blossoms), cut into two	40	g.	1 1/2	oz.
2	Tbsps.	Cooking oil	30	mL.	2	Tbsp.
2	pcs.	Tokwa (tofu), cubed	180	g.	6	oz.
4	cloves	Garlic, crushed	12	g.	2	tsps.
1/2	cup	Mama Sita's Barbecue Marinade	120	mL.	4	fl. oz.
2	tsps.	Vinegar	10	mL.	2	tsps.
3/4	cup	Water	190	mL.	6	fl. oz.
4	Tbsps.	Mama Sita's Oyster Sauce	60	mL.	2	fl. oz.
3	cups	Boiled rice	540	g.	3	cups
		For topping dahon ng sibuyas (spring onions) chopped for topping				

1. Wash the banana blossoms thoroughly and soak in a bowl of water for 5 minutes. Drain and squeeze out all the water.

2. In a small saucepan, combine vinegar, Mama Sita's Barbecue Marinade, water and the banana blossoms. Cook over medium heat until the banana blossoms are tender. (About 10-15 minutes.) Drain and reserve.

3. In a wok, heat the cooking oil and fry the tokwa until it is golden brown on all sides (about 7 to 10 minutes). Set aside the tokwa.

4. Using the same cooking oil, sauté the garlic until golden brown (2-3 minutes)

5. Add the Mama Sita's Oyster sauce, rice and banana blossoms.

6. Stir-fry until the oyster sauce and banana blossoms have thoroughly blended

7. Top with green onions.

   Serve hot.

A very unique meatless dish!

KANGKONG WITH OYSTER SAUCE

			Metric		English	
1	bundle	Kangkong (or any green leafy vegetables of your choice like spinach, pechay)	300	g.	10	oz.
2	Tbsp.	Cooking oil	30	mL.	1	fl. oz.
5	cloves	Garlic	15	g.		
2	Tbsps.	Mama Sita's Oyster Sauce	30	mL.	1	fl. oz.

1. Sauté the garlic and Mama Sita's Oyster Sauce.

2. Add kangkong and stir-fry.

   Serve hot.

VEGETABLES UNLIMITED

			Metric		English	
1/2 Kg.		Mixed vegetables (your choice of vegetables like sayote, green beans, carrots, cabbage, chicharo, etc.)	1/2 Kg.		9	oz.
6	Tbsps.	Mama Sita's Oyster Sauce	90	mL.	3	fl. oz.
1/2 cup		Onion, sliced	20	g.	1-1/4	oz.
3	cloves	Garlic, crushed	10	g.	3/4	tsp.
1	Tbsp.	Cornstarch dissolved in	1	Tbsp.	1	Tbsp.
1/2 cup		Water	1/2 cup		2	fl oz.
2	Tbsps.	Cooking oil	2	Tbsp.	2	Tbsps.

1. Sauté garlic and onion.

2. Add mixed vegetables. Stir and simmer until half-cooked.

3. Pour Mama Sita's Oyster Sauce. Stir fry.

4. Add cornstarch dissolved in water to thicken the sauce.

3

CHOPSUEY

Makes 4-6 servings.

			Metric		English	
1	cup	**Water**	250	mL.	8	fl. oz.
1	pouch	**Mama Sita's Chopsuey Mix**	40	g.	1 1/2 oz.	
3	Tbsps.	**Cooking oil**	45	mL.	1 1/2 fl.oz.	
230	g.	**Meat, thinly sliced or shrimps, shelled and deveined**	230	g.	8	oz.
1/2	Kg.	**Assorted vegetables, cut-up (carrots, celery, cauliflower cabbage, snow peas, mushrooms, etc.)**	1/2	Kg.	1	lb.
1	tsp.	**Mama Sita's Oyster Sauce (optional)**	5	mL.	1	tsp.
1	tsp.	**Sesame oil (optional)**	5	mL.	1	tsp.

1. *Dissolve Mama Sita's Chopsuey Mix in water. Set aside.*

2. *In a pan, fry meat or shrimp quickly over high heat.*

3. *Add assorted vegetables.*

4. *Stir in dissolved mix and cook for 3 minutes.*

5. *Serve hot.*

For Pancit Canton :

Drop 8 oz. (230 g.) canton noodles in 6 cup (1.5 li.) boiling water. Separate noodles with fork while cooking for 1 minute. Drain, let dry and set aside. Prepare chopsuey and stir in cooked noodles just before removing from fire.

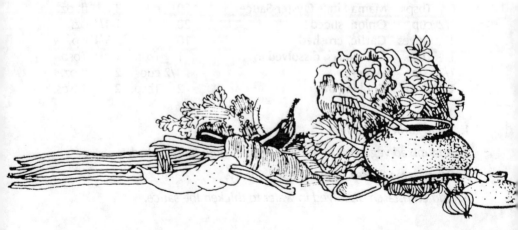

PANSIT BUKO WITH OYSTER SAUCE
(Young Coconut and Vegetable Stir Fry)

Makes 4 servings.

			Metric		English	
2	Tbsps.	Cooking oil	30	mL.	2	Tbsps .
6	cloves	Garlic, crushed	18	g.	3 1/2	tsps.
1	pc.	Onion, sliced	50	g.	2	oz.
1/2	cup	Carrots, strips	50	g.	2	oz.
3	Tbsps.	Mama Sita's Oyster Sauce	45	mL.	3	Tbsps.
1	cup	Cabbage, sliced thinly	60	g.	2	oz.
2	pcs.	Buko (young coconut), shredded	560	g.	18	oz.
1/2	tsp.	Patis (fish sauce)		1/2 tsp.	1/2 tsp.	
		Wansoy or coriander leaves, for garnishing				

1. Sauté garlic and onion.

2. Add the following: carrots, Mama Sita's Oyster Sauce, cabbage and buko.

3. Add the fish sauce.

4. Garnish with wansoy or coriander leaves.

5. Serve with kalamansi.

PINAKBET
(Tropical Vegetable Stew)

<u>Makes 4-6 servings</u>

			Metric	English
1	cup	Pork belly, cut into strips	200 g.	7 oz.
4	cloves	Garlic, crushed	12 g.	2 tsps.
1	pc.	Onion, sliced	50 g.	2 oz.
1	pc.	Tomato, sliced	50 g.	2 oz.
6	pcs.	Sitaw (string beans), cut 1" length	100 g.	3 oz.
3/4	cup	Okra, sliced	100 g.	3 oz.
1	cup	Kalabasa (squash or pumpkin), sliced	150 g.	5 oz.
1 1/2	cup	Eggplant, sliced	150 g.	5 oz
1	cup	Ampalaya (bitter melon)	120 g.	4 oz.
1/4	cup	Mama Sita's Palabok (Shrimp Gravy) Mix	50 g.	2 3/4 oz.
1	Tbsp.	Mama Sita's Oyster Sauce	15 mL.	1 Tbsp.
		Salt to taste		

1. In a pan, add just enough water to cover the pork. Cook over medium heat until the fat is rendered and fry until it is golden brown. Remove pork and set aside.

2. In the same pan, sauté garlic and onion.

3. Add the tomatoes and cooked pork.

4. Add the string beans, okra, squash, eggplant and bitter melon last.

5. Pour in Mama Sita's Palabok (Shrimp Gravy) Mix and Mama Sita's Oyster Sauce. Cover and continue to simmer stirring occassionally for 3 to 5 minutes or until vegetables are ready.

SPICY SITAW

<u>Makes 4 servings.</u>

			Metric		English	
1	tali	Sitaw (long green beans), cut into 1 inch (2 1/2 cm) pieces	250	g.	9	oz.
6	cloves	Garlic, crushed	20	g.	2	tsp.
1	pc.	Sili (chili pepper)	1	pc.	1	pc.
1	pc.	Onion, chopped	40	g.	1	oz.
1	Tbsp.	Bagoong (shrimp paste)	10	g.	1	Tbsp.
1/4	Kg.	Ground pork	250	g.	9	oz.
2	Tbsps.	Mama Sita's Barbecue Marinade	30	mL.	2	Tbsps.
1	Tbsp.	Gin	15	mL.	1/2	fl. oz.
		Sesame oil (optional)				

1. *Deep fry the sitaw, drain and set aside.*

2. *Sauté the onions, garlic and chilis.*

3. *Add the shrimp paste and stir-fry, pour in the gin.*

4. *Add the ground pork and stir-fry until cooked.*

5. *Pour in the Mama Sita's Barbecue Marinade.*

6. *Add the fried sitaw. Mix well.*

7. *Just before removing from fire, add a few drops of sesame oil.*

By now, bagoong, garlic and sitaw are all too familiar to us. But the way sitaw is cooked (deep fried) plus the addition of new ingredients (Barbecue Marinade and sesame oil) add a very interesting twist to this dish.

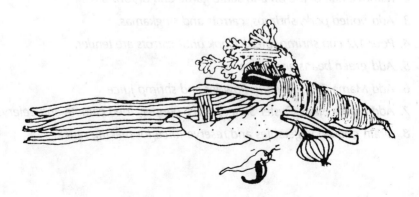

LUMPIANG GULAY
(Vegetable Rolls)

Makes 12 servings

			Metric		English	
2	cups	Camote, (sweet potato) or potato cut into strips	200	g.	7	oz.
1/4	cup	Cooking oil	60	mL.	2	fl oz.
5	cloves	Garlic, minced	15	g.	3	tsp.
1	pc.	Onion, sliced	60	g.	2	oz.
1	cup	Pork, boiled (reserve 1 cup soup stock) cut into strips	1/4	Kg.	9	oz.
1	cup	Shrimp, shelled (pound shrimp head, add 1 cup reserved stock, extract shrimp juice and strain) reserve juice	1/4	Kg.	9	oz.
2	cups	Singkamas, (jicama) cut into strips	200	g.	7	oz.
1	cup	Carrots, cut into strips	200	g.	7	oz.
2	cups	Green beans, cut into strips	180	g.	6	oz.
3	cups	Togue (mung bean sprout), rinsed and drained	200	g.	7	oz.
1/4	cup	Celery, chopped	30	g.	1	oz.
1	tsp.	Mama Sita's Annatto Powder, dissolved in	1	tsp.	1	tsp
1/2	cup	Shrimp juice	120	mL	4	fl.oz.
1/4	cup	Mama Sita's Oyster Sauce	60	mL.	2	oz.
1	tsp.	Fish sauce (patis)	5	mL.	1	tsp.
		Dash of pepper				
15-20	pcs.	Lumpia wrapper	15-20	pcs.	15-20	pcs.
15-20	pcs.	Letsugas (native lettuce)	15-20	pcs.	15-20	pcs.

1. *Fry camote in 1/4 cup oil and set aside.*

2. *Remove half of the oil and sauté garlic and onion.*

3. *Add boiled pork, shrimps, carrots and singkamas.*

4. *Pour 1/2 cup shrimp juice. Cook until carrots are tender.*

5. *Add green beans and togue.*

6. *Add Mama Sita's Annatto Powder and shrimp juice.*

7. *Add Mama Sita's Oyster Sauce, patis, pepper, fried camote and celery.*

8. *Drain cooked vegetables and reserve juice for making sauce.*

9. Measure 1/2 cup (125 ml.) of the lumpia sauce and mix it with the vegetables.

10. Wrap in lumpia wrapper with letsugas .

11. Serve the remainder of the sauce on the side.

Sauce :

			Metric		English	
1	cup	Water	250	mL.	8	fl oz.
6	Tbsps.	Mama Sita's Oyster Sauce	90	mL.	3	fl oz.
10	Tbsps.	Brown sugar	150	g.	10	fl oz.
2	Tbsps.	Cornstarch	20	g.	2	Tbsps.
1/2	cup	Reserved juice from drained vegetables	120	mL.	4	fl oz.
1/4	cup	Peanuts, ground	30	g.	1	oz.
1	tsp.	Garlic, chopped	1	tsp.	1	tsp.

1. In a saucepan, combine all ingredients except peanut and garlic. Stir over low heat until sauce thickens.

2. Mix the ground peanuts and crushed garlic to the sauce.

CREAMY ADOBO DIP

For a nutritious snack for children, wash, drain and chill fresh fruits and vegetables like sliced apples, carrots, cucumber, celery sticks or previously blanched mung bean sprouts.

Combine 1 1/2 Tbsps. Mama Sita's Savory Sauce (Adobo) Mix, 1 tsp. sugar and Sour Cream (8 oz.) and whip until well blended. Keep refrigerated until before serving.

Arrange chilled vegetables attractively in a serving bowl with dip at center.

TO MAKE HOME MADE SOUR CREAM

1	cup	Evaporated milk or all-purpose cream
1	Tbsp.	Calamansi juice

Mix 1 cup evaporated milk with 1 Tbsp. calamansi juice. Allow the mixture to stand until it curdles and thickens.

STIR-FRIED VEGETABLES WITH GARLIC SAUCE
(Garlic Vegetables)

Makes 4 servings.

		Metric		English	
1/2 cup	Carrots, sliced into thin discs	200	g.	7	oz.
1 1/2 cups	Button mushroom, quartered	200	g.	7	oz.
2 1/3 cups	Young chicharo (snow peas), stringed	250	g.	9	oz.

Garlic Sauce :

			Metric		English	
3	Tbsps.	Garlic, minced	45	g.	2	oz.
1	Tbsp.	Ginger, minced	15	g.	1	Tbsp.
	1/4 cup	Spring onion, minced	15	g.		1/4 cup
2	Tbsps.	Cooking oil	30	mL.	1	fl. oz.

Seasoning Sauce :

			Metric		English	
1 1/2 Tbsps.		Cornstarch	10	g.	1 1/2 Tbsp.	
1	Tbsps.	Mama Sita's Oyster Sauce	5	mL.	3	Tbsps.
	1/2 tsp.	Sesame oil	2.5	mL.	1/2 tsp.	
1 1/2 cups		Chicken broth	375	mL.	12	fl. oz.
1	tsp.	Salt	5	g.	1/2 tsp.	

1. Blanch the carrots, mushrooms and chicharo separately. Set aside.

2. Sauté garlic, ginger and spring onion in cooking oil.

3. Pour in the seasoning sauce.

4. Add the blanched vegetables and stir-fry until cooked.

PANSIT BIHON GUISADO
(Stir Fried Veggies Over Rice Noodles)

<u>Makes 8 servings</u>

			Metric		English	
1/2	Kg.	Bihon (rice noodles), wash quickly just before using	1/2	Kg.	1	lb.
1/4	Kg.	Pork, cut into strips	1/4	Kg.	9	oz.
2	pcs.	Tofu (tokwa), sliced 1/2" cubes	120	g.	4 1/4	oz.
1/4	Kg.	Shrimps, peeled (pound heads, add	1/4	Kg.	9	oz.
1/2	cup	Water, extract juice, reserve)	125	mL.	4	fl.oz.
1	pc.	Garlic, minced, fried, half of it reserved for garnishing	30	g.	2	Tbsps.
1/4	cup	Onion, sliced	20	g.	1/4	cup
1	cup	Baguio beans, strips	100	g.	3 1/2	oz.
1	cup	Snow peas (chicharo), remove stems and strings	100	g.	3 1/2	oz.
1	cup	Carrots, julienned	100	g.	3 1/2	oz.
2	cups	Cabbage, sliced thinly	100	g.	3 1/2	oz.
31/2	cups	Soup stock	875	mL.	28	fl.oz.
4	Tbsps.	Mama Sita's Oyster Sauce	60	mL.	2	fl.oz.
2	Tbsps.	Fish sauce (patis)	2	Tbsps.	2	Tbsps.
2	Tbsps.	Soy sauce	30	mL.	2	Tbsps.
2	tsps.	Sesame oil	10	mL.	2	tsps.
1/4	tsp.	Blackpepper	1/4	tsp.	1/4	tsp.
1/4	cup	Green onions, sliced thinly	15	g.	1/4	cup

1. In a pan, place pork and add a little water, simmer until the fat is rendered and fry in its own fat until brown. Set aside.

2. In the same pan, fry tofu until golden brown. Set aside.

3. Sauté garlic and onion. Add the shrimp. When the shrimp is cooked, add the soup stock, shrimp juice, Mama Sita's Oyster Sauce, patis and soy sauce.

4. Bring the soup stock to a boil and blanch the vegetables one at a time. Set aside the vegetables.

5. Add bihon and cook over medium fire until tender. Add half of the reserved cooked vegetables and mix thoroughly.

6. Season with pepper and sesame oil.

7. Place on a platter and garnish with the remaining vegetables, fried garlic and green onions, fried pork and tofu.

8. Serve with calamansi and fish sauce.

GINISANG TOGUE
(Sauteed Bean Sprouts)

<u>Makes 6 servings.</u>

			Metric	English
1/4	Kg.	Kasim (pork belly, cut into strips)	250 g.	9 oz.
2	pcs.	Tokwa (tofu), cut into cubes	120 g.	4 oz.
4	cloves	Garlic, crushed	12 g.	2 tsp.
1	pc.	Onion, sliced	40 g.	1 oz.
2	pcs.	Tomatoes, sliced	80 g.	2 oz.
3	cups	Togue (mung bean sprout), washed and drained	250 g.	9 oz.
2	Tbsps.	Mama Sita's Palabok Mix	30 g.	1 oz.
1	tsp.	Fish sauce (patis)	5 mL.	1 tsp.

1. In a pan, add just enough water to cover the pork. Cook over medium heat until the fat is rendered and fry until golden brown. Remove the pork and set aside.

2. In the same pan, fry tokwa until golden brown. Remove the fried tokwa from the pan and set aside.

3. Sauté the garlic , onion and tomatoes .

4. Add the fried pork, fried tokwa, bean sprouts and Mama Sita's Palabok Mix. Stir and season with fish sauce.

5. Simmer for 5 minutes or until done.

UKOY
(Shrimp Vegetable Fritters)

Makes about one dozen 2" fritters.

Batter :

			Metric	English
1/2	cup	All-purpose flour	75 g.	2 1/2 oz.
1/2	cup	Cornstarch	80 g.	2 3/4 oz.
3/4	cup	Cold water	180 mL.	6 fl. oz.
1/3	cup	Mama Sita's Shrimp Gravy (Palabok) Mix	50 g.	1 3/4 oz.
1	cup	Kalabasa (squash), shredded	150 g.	5 oz.
1/2	cup	Carrots, shredded	80 g.	3 oz.
1/4	cup	Leeks, minced	25 g.	1/4 cup
1	sq. pc.	Tokwa (tofu), cut into 1/2" cubes	60 g.	2 oz.
12	small	Shrimps, peeled and deveined (optional)	250 g.	9 oz.
		Cooking oil for frying		

Garlic Dipping Sauce :

			Metric	English
1	cup	vinegar	250 mL.	8 fl. oz.
2	Tbsps.	Fish sauce (patis)	30 mL.	2 Tbsps.
4	cloves	Garlic, crushed	20 g.	1 tsp.
		Dash of blackpepper		

1. **To prepare the Batter :**

   Pre-squeeze juice out of shredded vegetables. Set aside.

   In a mixing bowl, combine all-purpose flour, cornstarch, Mama Sita's Shrimp Gravy (Palabok) Mix and water. Stir in squash, carrots and leeks.

2. **To prepare the Garlic Dip :**

   In a bowl, combine vinegar, fish sauce, garlic and blackpepper. Let stand for at least 20 minutes. Reserve until needed.

3. **To form the fritters :**

   In a saucer, form batter mixture into small 2" patties. Top with a shrimp and 3 tofu cubes. Gently slide into preheated 350° F. (170° C) cooking oil and fry until golden brown, about 5 minutes. Drain off excess oil. Continue process until you use up the batter mixture.

   Serve hot with garlic dipping sauce.

To prevent the ukoy from becoming soggy, squeeze out all the liquid from the carrots and squash before combining with the rest of the ingredients.

SOTANGHON-BIHON GUISADO
(Stir Fried Noodles)

<u>Makes 8 servings</u>

			Metric		English	
4	cups	Soup stock (See page 56)	1	li.	1	quart
1/4	Kg.	Chicken breast, boiled & flaked	1/4	Kg.	9	oz.
4	cloves	Garlic, fried, half of it reserved for garnishing	12	g.	1	tsp.
1	pc.	Onion, sliced	60	g.	2	oz.
2/3	cup	Green beans (Baguio beans), strips	100	g.	3 1/2	oz.
1/2	cup	Carrots, strips	100	g.	3 1/2	oz.
1/4	cup	Celery, chopped	45	g.	1 1/2	oz.
1	cup	Chicharo (snow peas) remove string and stem	100	g.	3 1/2	oz.
3	cups	Cabbage, strips	250	g.	8 3/4	oz.
1/2	tsp.	Mama Sita's Annatto Powder	1/2	tsp.	1/2	tsp.
5	Tbsps.	Mama Sita's Oyster Sauce	75	mL.	2 1/2	fl.oz.
4	Tbsps.	Patis (fish sauce), add more if desired	60	mL.	2	fl.oz.
1	pack	Sotanghon (Mung bean noodle), soaked for 1 minute	100	g.	3 1/2	oz.
1	pack	Bihon (rice noodle) rinsed drained	250	g.	8 3/4	oz.
1/4	tsp.	Pepper	1/4	tsp.	1/4	tsp.
8	pcs.	Calamansi, halved	8	pcs.	8	pcs.

1. Prepare the soup stock (see page 56)

2. Sauté garlic and onion. Add green beans, carrots, celery, chicharo, cabbage, flaked chicken and Mama Sita's Annatto Powder. Simmer until half-cooked. Set aside.

3. In the same pan, add soup stock, Mama Sita's Oyster Sauce and patis. Let boil.

4. Add sotanghon and simmer.

5. Add bihon, mix and cook until done. Add half of reserved vegetables and dash with blackpepper.

6. Top with the remaining vegetables and reserved garlic.

6. Serve with calamansi.

Mama Sita's LETTUCE SALAD

Makes 2 servings.

			Metric		English	
1	head	Lettuce	200	g.	7	oz.

Croutons :

			Metric		Emglish	
2	slices	Loaf bread, cut into cubes and fried until crisp.	2	slices	2	oz.
3	strips	Bacon, pan fried, chopped	50	g.	2	oz.

Dressing :

			Metric		English	
1/2	cup	Corn oil	125	mL.	4	fl. oz.
1/2	cup	Vinegar	125	mL.	4	fl. oz.
1	tsp.	Mama Sita's Adobo Mix	1	tsp.	1	tsp.
1	tsp.	Garlic, chopped	5	g.	1	tsp.
1	tsp.	Sugar	5	g.	1	tsp.
1/2	tsp.	Pepper	2.5	g.	1/2	tsp.
1/2	tsp.	Salt	2.5	g.	1/2	tsp.
1	Tbsp.	Bellpepper, chopped	10	g.	1	Tbsp.
2	tsps.	Rhum	10	mL.	2	tsps.

1. Mix all ingredients for dressing in a bottle with a tight cover and shake vigorously. Serve on a separate bowl.

2. Wash lettuce in running water. Soak in ice cold water. Tear into bite sizes. Dry. Arrange on a platter.

3. Top with croutons and chopped bacon.

FRIED RICE WITH OYSTER SAUCE

Makes 4 servings

			Metric		English	
2	pcs.	Eggs, scrambled, cut into strips	2	pcs.	2	pcs.
1	tsp.	Mama Sita's Shrimp Gravy (Palabok) Mix	1	tsp.	1	tsp.
2 1/2	Tbsps.	Mama Sita's Oyster Sauce	40	mL.	2 1/2	Tbsps.
3/4	tsp.	Salt	3/4	tsp.	3/4	tsp.
6	cloves	Garlic, crushed	18	g.	3 1/2	cloves
3	Tbsps.	Cooking oil	45	mL.	3	Tbsps.
3	cups	Left-over boiled rice	540	g.	14	oz.
1/2 cup		Carrots, chopped	80	g.	2 1/2	oz.
1/2 cup		Green peas	80	g.	2 1/2	oz.

1. Dissolve salt and Mama Sita's Shrimp Gravy (Palabok) Mix in Mama Sita's Oyster Sauce.

2. Sauté garlic in cooking oil until golden brown and toss in left-over boiled rice until hot.

3. Add salt-Palabok Mix-Oyster Sauce mixture. Mix thoroughly.

4. Add the remaining ingredients one at a time : scrambled eggs, carrots, and green peas.

Optional : You can add 1/2 cup leftover roast pork or ham cut in strips or 1 cup diced cooked shrimps.

PECHAY FLOWERS
(best in November)

<u>Makes 4-6 servings.</u>

			Metric		English	
1/2	Kg.	Pechay flowers (cauliflower or or broccoli are good substitutes)	1/2	Kg.	17	oz.
1/4	Kg.	Shrimp (beef, pork, chicken or fish may be used)	1/4	Kg.	9	oz.
1	Tbsp.	Soy sauce	30	mL.	1	Tbsp.
1	tsp.	Cornstarch for shrimps	1	tsp.	1	tsp.
1	tsp.	Cornstarch dissolved in	1	Tbsp.	1	Tbsp.
1	Tbsp.	Water	15	mL.	1	Tbsp.
1/4	cup	Soup stock or water	60	mL.	2	fl.oz.
1/2	tsp.	Ginger, minced	3	g.	1/2	tsp.
1/2	tsp.	Garlic, minced	3	g.	1/2	tsp.
3	Tbsps.	Cooking oil (corn or soya oil)	45	mL.	3	Tbsps.
1	Tbsp.	Mama Sita's Oyster Sauce	15	mL.	1	Tbsp.
1	Tbsp.	Gin or rum (optional) White pepper to taste	15	mL.	1	Tbsp.

1. Combine salt, white pepper, cornstarch and gin or rum.

2. Roll shrimps in cornstarch mixture.

3. Heat wok and add cooking oil. Sauté minced ginger and garlic.

4. Add shrimps and stir fry until it turns pink.

5. Add vegetables, Mama Sita's Oyster Sauce and sugar.

5. Thicken with cornstarch dissolved in water.

6. Stir fry quickly until the vegetables are ready.

GINISANG MONGGO
(Sauteed Mung Beans)

			Metric		English	
1	cup	Kasim (pork belly) cut into strips	200	g.	7	oz.
1/2	cup	Monggo (mung beans) washed	60	g.	1/2	cup
4	cups	Water	1	Li.	1	quart
4	cloves	Garlic, crushed	12	g.	2	tsp.
1	pc.	Onion, sliced	60	g.	2	oz.
1	pc.	Ripe tomato, chopped	50	g.	2	oz.
2	Tbsps.	Mama Sita's Shrimp Gravy (Palabok) Mix dissolved in:	16	g.	2	Tbsps.
1/2	cup	Water	120	mL.	4	fl.oz.
1/2	cup	Ampalaya (bitter melon) leaves or malunggay leaves				
1	tsp.	Salt	1	tsp.	1	tsp.

1. Boil mung beans until done. Set aside.

2. In a wok, add just enough water to cover the pork. Cook over medium heat until the fat is rendered and fry the pork until it is golden brown.

3. Sauté garlic and onion.

4. Add tomato, fried pork and cooked mung beans. Stir and cover. Set to medium heat.

5. Add Mama Sita's Shrimp Gravy (Palabok) Mix and leaves. Cover and simmer until done.

FRIED BEAN CURD WITH OYSTER SAUCE

Makes 4 servings

			Metric	English
1	cup	Fresh button mushrooms, washed and sliced	120 g.	3 oz.
4	Tbsps.	Cooking oil	60 mL.	2 fl. oz.
5	sq. pcs.	Tokwa (tofu), cubed	500 g.	17 oz.
3	Tbsps.	Mama Sita's Oyster Sauce	45 mL.	3 Tbsps.
1/4	cup	Spring onions slice into 1/2" (1 cm) lengths	20 g.	1/4 cup

1. Heat the oil and fry the mushrooms over high heat for 2 minutes, stirring all the time. Remove the mushrooms from the pan and set aside.

2. In the same pan, cook the tokwa gently for 2-3 minutes or until it starts to form a golden brown crust.

3. Add the Mama Sita's Oyster Sauce and pepper, mix well and cook for another 2 minutes.

4. Add the mushrooms, and stir fry for another 3 to 5 minutes.

5. When the mushrooms start to wilt, add the spring onions and remove from heat.

6. Serve immediately.

Seafoods

*"I started with the sinigang na hipon ...
It was full of flavor and had kangkong,
whole green chilis and Chinese radish.
The sourish taste was not overpower-
ing, it was tangy and whetted the
appetite.*

*On the whole, the meal at $12.50 ++
per person, was a taste-opener"*

– Kung Eu Meng
The Strait Times, Singapore
November 19, 1987

TOM YUM GOONG
(Lemon Grass Soup)

Makes 6 servings.

			Metric		English	
6	cups	Water	1.5	li.	3	pints
1/4 Kg		Shrimps, shelled (set aside heads & shells)	1/4	Kg.	9	oz.
1	Tbsp.	Fish sauce	15	mL.	1	Tbsp.
3	Tbsps.	Mama Sita's Biglang Sinigang	3	Tbsps.	3	Tbsps.
1	med. pc.	Onion, quartered	50	g.	1 1/2	oz.
2	med. pcs.	Tomatoes, quartered	100	g.	3	oz.
1	tsp.	Salt	1	tsp.	1	tsp.
		Wansoy (coriander leaves)				
2	stalks	Tanglad (lemon grass)	30	g.	1	oz.

1. Bring the water to a rolling boil. Drop in the shrimp heads and shells.

2. Boil for 5 minutes.

3. Strain the stock and discard the shrimp heads and shells.

4. Add the fish sauce, Mama Sita's Biglang Sinigang, shrimps, onions, tomatoes and lemon grass. Simmer until the vegetables are tender.

5. Garnish with wansoy.

Very refreshing!

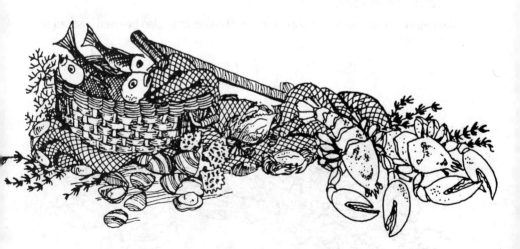

SINIGANG NA HIPON
(Shrimps in Tamarind Broth)

Makes 8 servings

			Metric		English	
5	cups	Water	1/4	li.	40	fl.oz.
1	med.	Onion, peeled and quartered	100	g..	3 1/2	oz.
1	large	Tomato, quartered	100	g.	3 1/2	oz.
1	6"	Labanos (radish), peeled and cut into 1/4" diagonal slices	200	g.	7	oz.
1	cup	String beans, cut into 2" strips	100	g.	3 1/2	oz.
2	pcs.	Green chili pepper	20	g.		
1	pouch	Mama Sita's Tamarind Seasoning Mix (Pang-Sinigang)	25	g.	7/8	oz.
20-25	pcs.	Shrimps,	1/2	Kg.	1.1	lb.
1	cup	Green leafy vegetables (like kangkong, spinach or mustard greens)	50	g.	2	oz.
1/2	Tbsp.	Fish sauce (patis)	7	mL.	1/2	Tbsp.

1. Bring water to a boil. Add onion, tomato and labanos. Simmer for 5 minutes.

2. Add string beans, chili pepper, fish sauce, and Mama Sita's Tamarind Seasoning Mix (Pang Sinigang). Continue to simmer for 3 minutes uncovered.

3. Add the shrimps, simmer for another 3 minutes. Turn off the heat, add leafy green vegetables. Cover to steam cook leafy vegetables.

Serve immediately.

Variation : Fish, pork or pre-boiled beef brisket may also be used instead of shrimps.

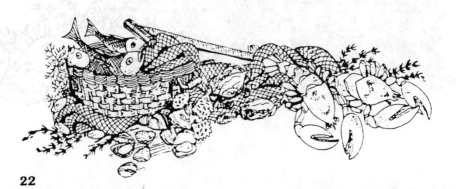

SEAFOOD CHOWDER

Makes 4 servings.

			Metric		English	
1/2 Kg.	Clams		1/2	Kg.	1	lb.
1 Tbsp.	Garlic, chopped finely		15	g.	1	Tbsp.
1/4 cup	Onion, chopped finely		50	g.	2	oz.
2 Tbsps.	Leeks, chopped finely		40	g.	2	Tbsps.
2/3 cup	Carrots, diced		100	g.	3	oz.
3/4 cup	Milk		200	mL.	6	fl. oz.
1 cup	Water		250	mL.	8	fl. oz.
1 piece	Bay leaf		1	pc..	1	pc.
1/4 cup	Mama Sita's Shrimp Gravy (Palabok) Mix		50	g.	60	mL.
1 tsp.	Grated orange rind (optional)		1	tsp.	1	tsp.

1. Soak the clams in water for several hours. Discard the sandy water.

2. Place clams in saucepan and add just enough water to cover. Boil.

3. When the clams open, turn off the heat.

4. Set aside 1 1/2 cups of the clam stock and discard the rest.

5. Sauté onions, leeks, carrots and bay leaf.

6. Add the clam stock and garlic, milk, and Mama Sita's Shrimp Gravy (Palabok) Mix.

7. Keep on stirring until the soup starts to thicken.

8. Add the clams and grated orange rind.

Chunks of Lapu-Lapu (snapper), mussels, crabs and shrimps may also be combined with the clams.

To make this soup even more interesting and flavorful, place a slice of toasted bread topped with garlic flavored mayonaise in a bowl. Pour the soup over it.

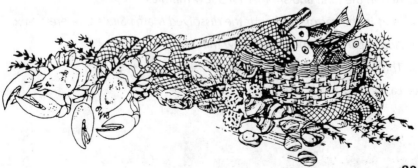

TUNA EMPANADA

Makes 50 pieces.

Filling:

			Metric		English	
2	Tbsps.	Cooking oil	30	mL.	2	Tbsp.
1	Tbsp.	Garlic, minced	15	g.	1	Tbsp.
1	med-sized	Onion, finely chopped	60	g.	2	oz.
2	cans	Tuna, canned, flaked	370	g.	13	oz.
3	Tbsps.	Mama Sita's Spicy Sauce (Caldereta) Mix dissolved in:	45	g.	3	Tbsps.
1/2	cup	Water	120	mL.	4	fl. oz.
1	tsp.	Sugar	3	g.	1	tsp.
1 1/2	Tbsps.	Cornstarch	15	g.	1 1/2	Tbsps.
1 1/2	tsp.	Water	7	mL.	1 1/2	tsp.
1/2	cup	Sweet peas , pre-cooked	85	g.	3	oz.
1/4	cup	Carrots, chopped	50	g.	2	oz.

Crust:

12	Tbsps.	Shortening	130	g.	5	fl. oz.
2 1/2	cups	All-purpose flour	370	g.	13	oz.
1	Tbsp.	Salt	15	g.	1	Tbsp.
2	Tbsps.	Sugar	20	g.	2	Tbsps.
10	Tbsps.	Ice-cold water	150	mL.	5	fl. oz.

Eggwash:

1	pc.	Eggyolk
1	Tbsp.	Butter, melted

Filling:

1. *Sauté the garlic and onion in oil.*
2. *Add in the tuna and simmer for a few minutes.*
3. *Add in the carrots and pour the dissolved Mama Sita's Caldereta Mix.*
4. *Add sugar and simmer for a few minutes.*
5. *Thicken mixture with dissolved cornstarch.*
6. *Lastly, add in the sweet peas.*

Crust:

1. *Add the shortening to flour, mix with salt and sugar, and cut it with pastry blender until grainy.*

2. *Add enough water to form into ball.*

3. *Roll out the dough and cut into 1 1/2" round pieces.*

To Assemble the Empanada:

1. *Put about 1 teaspoonful of the prepared filling at the center of each piece of crust.*

2. *Fold it forming half-moon shape pieces. Wet the sides with a little water to seal completely.*

3. *Flute the sides and arrange them on a cookie sheet.*

4. *Brush top with eggwash and bake at 350° F. for about 30 minutes.*

Eggwash:

Mix together the egg yolk and melted butter

Note: Tuna can be substituted with ground pork or boiled chicken (300 g. per recipe)

PAELLA PILIPINA

Makes 8 servings :

			Metric		English	
1	cup	Malagkit (glutinous) rice	250	g.	1/2	lb.
1 1/2	cups	Long grain rice	350	g.	12	oz.
5	cups	Chicken stock	1 1/4	li.	2 1/2	pints
1	tsp.	Mama Sita's Annatto Powder All-Natural Food Color	5	g.	1	tsp.
2	Tbsps.	Olive oil or vegetable oil	30	mL.	1	fl. oz.
1	pc.	Chorizo (Spanish sausage) cut into 1/2" diagonal slices	100	g.	3	oz.
230	g.	Shrimp, peeled and deveined	230	g.	8	oz.
7	pcs.	Baby squid, cut into 1/4" diagonal rings	230	g.	8	oz.
1	tsp.	Minced garlic	5	g.	1	tsp.
1	med.	Chopped onions	100	g.	3	oz.
2	med.	Tomatoes, cored and chopped	100	g.	3	oz.
1	med.	Red bell pepper, cored, seeded, minced	100	g.	3	oz.
1	Tbsp.	Patis (Fish sauce)	15	mL.	1	Tbsp.
3	Tbsps.	Mama Sita's Spicy Sauce (Caldereta) Mix	30	g.	1	oz.
2	med.	Blue crabs, split in halves	250	g.	9	oz.
230	g.	Mussels	230	g.	8	oz.
230	g.	Clams	230	g.	8	oz.
1	med.	Green bellpepper, cored, seeded and julienned	100	g.	3	oz.
2/3	cup	Green peas	100	g.	3	oz.
1	pc.	Hard boiled egg, cut into thin round slices	1	pc	1	pc.
		Dahon ng sibuyas (spring onion) chopped for garnish.				

1. _In a pot, combine the glutinous and long grain rice. Rinse twice. Drain. Return to pot and add 4 1/2 cup chicken stock and Annatto Powder. Stir until well blended. Bring to a boil, lower to a simmer, cover and cook until done about 20 minutes. Turn off heat and allow to cool for at least 10 minutes._

2. Meanwhile in a paellera or a large sauté pan, heat oil. Sauté chorizo for one minute. Reserve. Sauté shrimp for about 2-3 minutes. Reserve. Add squid, sauté for 1 minute or just until it changes color from opaque to milky white.

3. In the same pan over high heat, sauté garlic and onion for 30 seconds. Add tomatoes, minced red pepper and sauté for 1 minute.

4. Add fish sauce (patis), remaining 1/2 cup stock and Mama Sita's Spicy Sauce (Caldereta) Mix. Bring mixture to a boil, then lower and arrange crabs on top. Cover and simmer for 5 minutes.

5. Add mussels and clams. Continue to simmer for another 3 minutes or until shells, are open. Remove cover.

6. Stir in julienned green bell peppers and peas. Cook the mixture for another minute.

7. To finish, add the Annatto rice, reserved chorizo, shrimp and squid. Toss until the mixture is well blended. Garnish top with boiled egg and spring onions, if desired. Serve hot.

SAUCY CLAMS

			Metric		English	
1	Kg.	Halaan (clams), cleaned	1	Kg.	2.2	lbs.
6	cloves	Garlic, crushed	18	g.	1	Tbsp.
2	Tbsps.	Mama Sita's Oyster Sauce	30	mL.	2	Tbsp.
2	Tbsps.	Green onion, sliced	10	g.	2	Tbsps.
2	Tbsps.	Cooking oil	30	mL.	1	fl. oz.
1/2 cup		Water	120	mL.	4	fl. oz.
2	sprigs	Wansoy (fresh coriander leaves)	5	g.		

1. Soak the clams in water for 30 minutes. Discard the sandy water.

2. Sauté garlic and onion.

3. Add Mama Sita's Oyster Sauce, clams, water and green onions.

4. Cook over medium heat until the clams are open.

5. Garnish with wansoy.

SWEET AND SOUR FISH

Makes 4 servings.

			Metric		English	
3	Tbsps.	Cooking oil	45	mL.	3	Tbsps,
3	cloves	Garlic, crushed	9	g.	1 2/3 tsp.	
2	pcs.	Onion, sliced	20	g	4	oz.
2	Tsps.	Ginger, thinly sliced	10	g.	2	Tsps.
1/2 med. pc.		Carrot, sliced into discs	50	g.	1 1/2 oz.	
1	med. pc.	Bell pepper, cubed (optional)	50	g.	1 1/2 oz.	
8	pcs.	Peppercorn, whole	8	pcs.	1	tsp.
1	pouch	Mama Sita's Sweet & Sour Sauce Mix dissolved in	57	g.	2	oz.
1 1/2 cup		Water	375	mL.	12	fl. oz.
3	pcs.	Fried whole fish or fish steak Salt to taste	1/2 Kg.	17	oz.	

1. Sauté garlic, onion, ginger, peppercorns carrots and bell pepper in cooking oil until half cooked.

2. Pour in the Mama Sita's Sweet and Sour Sauce Mix and water.

3. Stir until thick (about 5 minutes)

4. Add the fish and and simmer for 2 minutes.

   Serve hot.

RELLENONG BANGUS

Makes 4-6 servings.

			Metric		English	
2	pcs.	Bangus (milkfish)	1	Kg.	2.2	lbs.
1/4	cup	Mama Sita's Oyster Sauce	60	mL.	2	fl. oz.
3	pcs.	Kalamansi juice	15	mL.	1	Tbsp.
1	cup	Water	250	mL.	8	fl.oz.
2	Tbsps.	Cooking oil	30	mL.	1	fl. oz.
2/3	cup	Onion, chopped finely	80	g.	3	oz.
2/3	cup	Carrots, chopped finely	100	g.	4	oz.
3/4	cup	Potatoes, chopped finely	100	g.	4	oz.
1/2	cup	Green peas	85	g.	3	oz.
1/3	cup	Raisins	50	g.	2	oz.
2	pcs.	Eggs, beaten	2	pcs.	2	pcs.
2	cups	Cooking oil, for deep frying	500	mL.	16	fl. oz.

1. _Clean and scale the fish. Place the fish on a flat surface. Pound the body with the back of a knife or a mallet. Press your left hand firmly against the tail with your right hand and jerk it upward. The idea is to break the middle bone of the fish. With a spoon scrape out all the flesh and set it aside. Discard the middle bone of the fish._

2. _Combine the Mama Sita's Oyster Sauce with the kalamansi juice. Marinate the fish skin in the oyster sauce and kalamansi juice for 30 minutes._

3. _Boil the water, add the scraped fish meat and cook just until it turns white. Drain and pick out the bones._

4. _Sauté the onions in cooking oil. Add the carrots, potatoes, and green peas. Stir._

5. _When the vegetables are tender, add the fishmeat, oyster sauce and kalamansi, and raisins._

6. _Remove from heat and add the beaten eggs._

7. _Stuff this mixture into the fish skin until it reaches the neck. Deep fry until fish is golden brown._

8. _Serve hot._

Variation: Wrap in banana leaf or aluminum foil and bake at 325° F. for 45 minutes.

STUFFED SQUID

			Metric		English	
1	Kg.	Squid, cleaned	1	Kg.	2.2	lb.
1	cup	Mama Sita's Barbecue Marinade	250	mL.	8	fl. oz.
1	cup	Cooking oil	250	mL.	8	fl. oz.

Stuffing :

			Metric		English	
1/2	Kg.	Shrimp, shelled, chopped	1/2	Kg.	17	oz.
1/2	Kg.	Ground pork	1/2	Kg.	17	oz.
1	pouch	Mama Sita's Barbecue Marinade Mix	50	g.	1	pouch
4	slices	Bread, finely chopped and soaked in	4	slices	4	slices
1/4	cup	Milk	60	mL.	2	oz.
2	pcs.	Egg, beaten	2	pcs.	2	pcs.
1	pc.	Onion, finely chopped	60	g.	2	oz.
1/3	cup	Celery, finely chopped	40	g.	1/3	cup
2	Tbsps.	Green onion, finely chopped	40	g.	1/3	cup
2	tsps.	Iodized salt	2	tsps.	2	tsps.

Sauce :

			Metric		English	
2	Tbsps.	Garlic, chopped	2	Tbsps.	2	Tbsps.
1	pc.	Green onion, minced	60	g.	2	oz.
1	Tbsp.	Mama Sita's Oyster Sauce	1	Tbsp.	1	Tbsp.
1	tsp.	Sesame oil	1	tsp.	1	tsp.

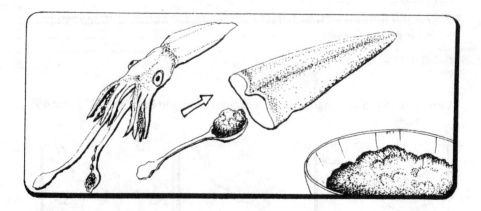

1. Marinate squid in Mama Sita's Barbecue Marinade for 30 minutes, turning occasionally.

2. Combine all ingredients for stuffing. Mix well and chill for 30 minutes.

3. Fill the squid with stuffing well up to the neck. Replace heads and fasten with a toothpick to keep it in place.

4. Place the squid in a shallow pan and simmer with the marinade for 20 minutes.

5. Reserve the stock and and fry the squid for about 5 minutes. Drain off excess oil.

6. In the same pan where the squid was fried, remove some of the oil and sauté garlic and green onion.

7. Pour reserved stock and Mama Sita's Oyster Sauce. Simmer for 2 minutes.

8. Add the sesame oil and remove from heat.

9. Pour the sauce over the stuffed squid and serve.
(Do not forget to remove the toothpick before serving.)

Variation :

1. Follow steps 1 to 3.

2. Set oven to 300° F.

3. Place the squid in the baking pan and bake for 25-30 minutes. Brush with the marinade-cooking oil mixture occasionally.

3. Deglaze the squid drippings from the baking pan with 1/2 cup water.

4. In 2 tablespoons oil, sauté the garlic and green onion.

5. Add the squid drippings and Mama Sita's Oyster Sauce. Simmer for 2 minutes.

6. Add the sesame oil and remove from heat.

7. Pour the sauce over the stuffed squid and serve.

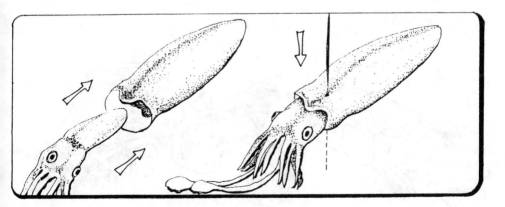

ADOBONG PUSIT
(Squid Adobo)

<u>Makes 4 servings</u>

			Metric		English	
approx. 6 med. size		Squid, cleaned (Remove inkbag and dilute in 1/4 cup (60 ml.) water Reserve.)	1/2	Kg.	1	lb.
2	Tbsps.	Mama Sita's Oyster Sauce	30	mL.	2	Tbsps.
2	Tbsps.	Mama Sita's Barbecue Marinade	30	mL.	2	Tbsps.
1	tsp.	Ginger, minced	5	g.	1	tsp.
1	pc.	Onion, coarsely chopped	40	g.		1/2 cup
3	Cloves	Garlic, crushed	10	g.		1 2/3 tsp.
1	Tbsp.	Vinegar	15	mL.	1	Tbsp.
1/4	tsp	Salt	1/4	tsp.		1/4 tsp.
1	sprig	Kutsay (chives), minced	1	sprig	1	sprig

Dash   ground blackpepper

1. *Sauté garlic, ginger and onion.*

2. *Add the squid. Stir fry.*

3. *Pour in the Mama Sita's Oyster Sauce and Mama Sita's Barbecue Marinade . When it boils, remove the squid from the pan (do not overcook the squid).*

4. *Add the ink and water mixture. Simmer with constant stirring until the sauce thickens.*

5. *Put back the squid into the pan and simmer. When it boils, turn off the fire.*

6. *Serve with rice.*

GARLIC SQUID

			Metric		English	
12	med. pcs.	Pusit (*squid*) cleaned and washed	400	g.	14	oz.
1/2	tsp.	Ginger, minced	2	g.	1/2	tsp.
6	cloves	Garlic, crushed	20	g.	4	tsps.
1/3	cup	Leeks, chopped	30	g.	1	oz.
1/4	cup	Mama Sita's Oyster Sauce	60	mL.	2	fl. oz.
1	Tbsp.	Wansoy (*cilantro* or coriander leaves dash of sesame oil (optional)	20	g.	1	Tbsp.

1. Sauté the garlic, before it turns golden, add the ginger and the leeks.

2. Add the Mama Sita's Oyster Sauce.

3. Add the squid, stir fry until cooked.

4. Add a few drops of sesame oil (if you like).

5. Garnish with wansoy.

SPICY SIZZLING SHRIMPS

Makes 2 servings.

			Metric		English	
200	g.	Prawns Salt and pepper to season	200	g.	7	oz.
1	Tbsp.	Garlic, crushed	20	g.	1	Tbsp.
2	Tbsps.	Chinese wine	30	mL.	2	Tbsps.
1	Tbsp.	Garlic, sliced	20	g.	1	Tbsp.
2	Tbsps.	Corn oil	30	mL.	2	Tbsps.
1/4	cup	Mama Sita's Oyster Sauce, diluted in	60	mL.	2	fl.oz.
1/2	cup	Water	120	mL.	4	fl. oz.
1	Tbsp.	Cornstarch	10	g.	1	Tbsp.
1/2	tsp.	Sugar	1/2	tsp.	1/2	tsp.
1/4	cup	Sweet peas	40	g.	1/4	cup
1	pc.	Red chili pepper, sliced	50	g.	1/4	cup

1. Season the shrimps with salt and pepper. Marinate it with crushed garlic and Chinese wine for several minutes. Set aside.

2. Toast the sliced garlic in oil until golden brown.

3. Add the marinated shrimps and pan-fry until it turns pink.

4. Pour in the Mama Sita's Oyster Sauce mixed with water, cornstarch and sugar. Simmer for a few minutes, then add the sweet peas and chili pepper.

5. Transfer mixture on a hot plate and serve right away - sizzling!

PINANGAT SA GATA
(Fish Poached in Coconut Sauce)

<u>Makes 6 servings.</u>

			Metric		English	
1/2 Kg.		Fish (sliced tuna, hasa-hasa, or sapsap)	1/2 Kg.		1	lb.
1	Tbsp.	Mama Sita's Sinigang Mix dissolved in	15	g.	1	Tbsp.
1/2 cup		Water	120	mL.	4	fl.oz.
2	tsps.	Fish sauce (patis)	10	mL.	2	tsps.
1	cup	gata (coconut milk)	250	ml.	8	fl.oz

1. Combine all ingredients in a saucepan and bring to a boil.

2. Lower the heat and simmer until the fish is almost done.

3. Add the coconut milk and continue cooking until the coconut milk turns oily. Remove from heat immediately and serve with rice.

TOCINO'NG ISDA

<u>Makes 4 servings.</u>

			Metric		English	
2	pcs.	Fish: Bangus (milkfish), Carp or Trout	1/2 Kg.		17	oz.
1	pouch	Mama Sita's Marinating (Tocino) Mix	75	g.	2 2/3`	oz.

1. Slit fish on the back side from head to tail, wash and pat dry.

2. Sprinkle Mama Sita's Marinating (Tocino) Mix on the fish and rub it evenly on the flesh.

3. Marinate for at least 15 minutes.

4. Pan fry over medium heat.

Discover a new way to treat fish!

CRAB LUMPIA
(Crab Rolls)

<u>Makes 4 servings.</u>

			Metric		English	
1/4	Kg.	Crabmeat	1/4	Kg.	9	oz.
2	Tbsps.	Sibuyas Tagalog (Spring onion), finely chopped	20	g.	2	Tbsps.
2	Tbsps.	Mama Sita's Barbecue Marinade Mix	30	mL.	2	Tbsps.
1/2	tsp.	Salt	1/2	tsp.	1/2	tsp.
1	pc.	Egg, beaten	1	pc.	1	pc.
1	pc.	Onion, finely chopped	60	g.	2	oz.
2	Tbsps.	Cornstarch	20	g.	2	Tbsps.
1	tsp.	Sesame oil	5	mL.	1	tsp.
20	pcs.	Lumpia (spring roll) pastry wrapper Cooking oil, for deep frying	20	pcs.	20	pcs.

<u>Dipping Sauce:</u>

			Metric		English	
1	pouch	Mama Sita's Sweet and Sour Sauce Mix	57	g.	2	oz.
3/4	cup	Water	180	mL.	6	oz.

1. Combine crabmeat, spring onion, Barbecue Mix, salt, egg, cornstarch and sesame oil. Chill for 30 minutes.

2. Spoon one tablespoon of the mixture onto the lumpia wrapper.

3. Brush the edges with eggwhites or water and roll tightly to seal.

4.. Deepfry.

Dipping Sauce : (see page 36)

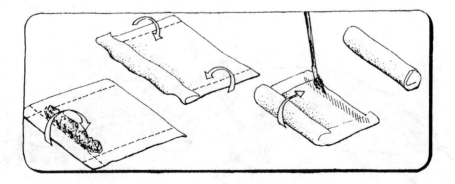

CALAMARES
(Squid Rings)

Makes 4 servings.

			Metric		English	
8	pcs.	Pusit (squid),	1/2	Kg.	1	lb.
1	pc.	Calamansi	1	pc.	1	pc.
1	pouch	Mama Sita's Sweet and Sour				
		Sauce Mix	57	g.	2	oz.
1/2	cup	Mama Sita's Palabok Mix	70	g.	2.5	oz.
1	cup	Cornstarch	120	g.	5.6	oz.

1. *Clean the squid, remove head, cut into rings about 1/8" thick.*

2. *Squeeze calamansi over the squid then wash thoroughly. Drain.*

3. *Combine Mama Sita's Palabok Mix and cornstarch.*

4. *Roll squid rings lightly in the palabok-cornstarch mixture.*

5. *Deep fry until golden brown.*

6. *Serve with Mama Sita's Sweet and Sour Sauce or vinegar with crushed garlic, salt and pepper.*

Dipping Sauce :

1. *Dissolve 1 pouch (57 g.) Mama Sita's Sweet and Sour Sauce Mix in 3/4 cup water.*

2. *Boil and simmer, stirring constantly for 2 minutes.*

Variation : For more fruity flavor, substitute 3/4 cup water with any of the following :

a. 3/4 cup Orange juice

b. 1/2 cup Pineapple juice and 1/4 cup water mixed with juice from 4 pieces calamansi juice or 1 lemon diluted with 3/4 cup water.

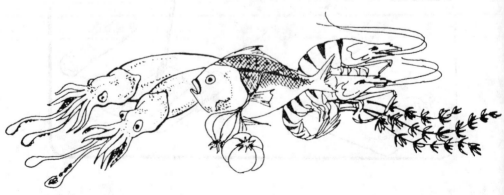

36

STEAMED LAPU-LAPU

<u>Makes 6 servings.</u>

			Metric		English	
2	med. pcs.	Lapu-lapu, trimmed	1	Kg.	2.2	lbs.
1/2 cup		Mama Sita's Barbecue Marinade	120	mL.	4	fl. oz.
1/4 cup		Mama Sita's Oyster Sauce	60	mL.	2	fl. oz.
2	Tbsps.	Brown sugar	30	g.	2	Tbsps.
2	Tbsps.	Soy sauce	30	mL.	2	Tbsps.
1/4 cup		Water	120	mL.	4	fl. oz.
1	tangkay	Wansoy	20	g.	1	oz.
2	Tbsps.	Ginger	40	g.	1	oz.
2	Tbsps.	Garlic	40	g.	1	oz.
2	Tbsps.	Cooking oil	30	mL.	2	Tbsps.
		Dash of sesame oil				

1. Stuff the stomach of fish with slices of ginger and rub the skin with salt.

2. Steam or bake the fish until cooked.

3. Fry the garlic until golden brown and set aside.

4. Fry the ginger until crispy and set aside.

5. Combine barbecue marinade, oyster sauce, brown sugar, soy sauce, water and cooking oil used in frying the garlic and ginger. Simmer over medium heat until the sugar has dissolved.

6. Add sesame oil to the sauce.

7. Place the steamed fish on a platter, pour the sauce over it and top with fried ginger and garlic and wansoy leaves.

Freshest fish is essential, gather ingredients on hand and you're all set for an unforgettable dining experience.

HAKAW
(Half Moon Dumplings)

Makes 32 pieces

Filling :

			Metric		English	
15	pcs.	Shrimps, shelled and chopped	300	g.	11	oz.
1/2	cup	Singkamas (jicama)	50	g	2	oz.
3	cloves	Garlic, minced	9	g.	2	tsps.
2	Tbsps.	Pork fat, minced	50	g.	2	oz.
1	sprig	Spring onion				
3	sprigs	Wansoy (Fresh Coriander), chopped	3	sprigs	3	sprigs
1	Tbsp.	Mama Sita's Oyster Sauce	15	mL.	1	Tbsp.
1/2	tsp.	Salt	1/2	tsp.	1/2	tsp.
1/2		Eggwhite	1/2		1/2	
1/2	tsp.	Sesame oil	1/2	tsp.	1/2	tsp.
1/2	tsp.	White pepper	1/2	tsp.	1/2	tsp.
1/2	Tbsp.	Tengang daga, (wood ear mushroom) soaked and chopped	1/2	Tbsp.	1/2	Tbsp.

Dumpling Wrapper :

			Metric	English		
1	cup	Ting Mi Flour (Tapioca Flour)	140	g.	5	oz.
1	tsp .	Cornstarch	4	g.	1	tsp.
1/2	tsp.	Salt	1/2	tsp.	1/2	tsp.
1	Tbsp.	Cooking oil	15	mL.	1	Tbsp.
1/2	cup +					
2	Tbsps.	Water	155	mL.	5	fl. oz.

1. In a mixing bowl, combine all ingredients for the filling. Mix well, cover and chill.

2. Combine the flour and cornstarch.

3. In a small saucepan, combine the cooking oil with water and bring to a rolling boil. Remove from heat.

4. Gradually pour cooking oil and water over the flour. Working quickly, use a fork to stir the mixture until it forms a sticky mass. Cover the dough and let stand for 15 minutes, or until cool enough to handle.

5. Lightly oil a work surface and knead the dough for 5 minutes, or until smooth.

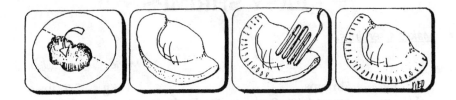

6. Divide the dough into 2 equal parts. Work with half of the dough at a time. Keep the other half covered with a damp cloth. Dust the work surface with flour. Knead each half of the dough for a few more minutes until very smooth. Roll the dough into your hand to form a long rope about 1 inch in diameter. Cut each rope into 16 equal portions.

7. Cover the dough pieces with a damp cloth as you work. Working with 1 portion at a time, roll out each piece of dough into 3 1/4" circle. Use a 3" cookie cutter to make a perfect round shape.

8. To form each dumpling, place a heaping teaspoon of the filling on one half of the dough circle.

9. Fold the dough over the filling and pinch the edges together to seal. Set the dumpling on the oiled tray and keep covered with a damp cloth.

10. Steam for 7-9 minutes until done.

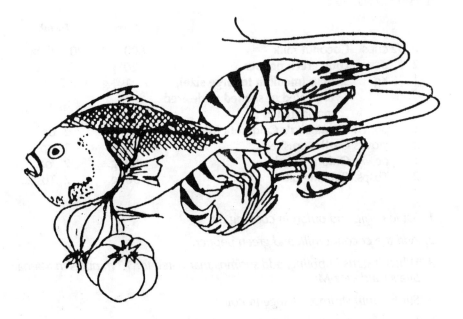

EASY SHRIMPS

Makes 4 servings.

		Metric		English
1 Kg.	Shrimps	1 Kg.	2.2	lbs.
1/2 cup	Mama Sita's Barbecue Marinade	125 mL.	4	fl.oz.
2 Tbsps.	Cooking oil	30 mL.	2	Tbsps.

1. Marinate shrimps in Mama Sita's Barbecue Marinade for 30 minutes.
2. Drain and reserve marinade.
3. Stir-fry shrimps in hot oil.
4. Add the Barbecue Marinade.
5. When the sauce starts to boil, remove from heat.

   Serve hot.

Kids love this!!

GUINATAANG HIPON
(Shrimps in Coconut Sauce)

Makes 4-6 servings.

		Metric		English
2 1/2 cups	Coconut milk	600 mL.	20	fl.oz.
2 pcs.	Long green pepper	20 g.	2	pcs.
1 Kg.	Shrimp (medium to large size), unpeeled or shelled as desired marinated in :	1 Kg.	2.2	lbs.
1 pouch	Mama Sita's Caldereta Mix	50 g.	2	oz.
2 cloves	Garlic, crushed	6 g.	1	tsp.
1 pc.	Onion, sliced	50 g.	2	oz.
2 Tbsps.	Cooking oil	30 g.	2	Tbsps.

1. Sauté garlic and onion in cooking oil.
2. Add the coconut milk and green pepper.
3. When it starts bubbling, add shrimps marinated for 15 minutes in Mama Sita's Caldereta Mix.
4. Stir fry until shrimps change in color.

When served over a bed of deep fried bihon (rice noodles), this makes a very simple yet interesting party dish.

40

SPECIAL PANCIT PALABOK
(Noodles with Shrimp Gravy)

<u>Makes 6 servings.</u>

			Metric		English	
200	g.	Palabok Noodles	200	g.	7	oz.
1/4	Kg.	Ground pork	250	g.	1/2	lb.
1	head	Garlic, crushed	10	g.	1	Tbsp.
3	Tbsps.	Cooking oil	45	mL.	3	Tbsps.
1	pouch	Mama Sita's Palabok (Shrimp Gravy) Mix	57	g.	2	oz.
12	cups	Soup stock to boil noodles	3	li.	3	quarts
3	cups	Soup stock (for the sauce)	3/4li.		1 1/2	pint
8	pcs.	Calamansi (sliced crosswise)				
		Fish sauce (patis) to taste				

<u>Garnishing</u>

			Metric		English	
1/4	cup	Crushed chicharon	17	g.	4	Tbsps.
2	Tbsps.	Deboned tinapa (smoked fish)	25	g.	2	Tbsps.
2	pcs.	Hard boiled eggs, sliced			2	pcs.
6	pcs.	Shrimps, boiled, shelled and halved	45	g.	3	oz.
2	pcs.	Kamias sliced thinly or	2	pcs.	2	pcs.
1	pc.	Sour star fruit (balimbing)	1	pc.	1	pc.
2	tsps.	Crushed garlic, fried	2	tsps.	2	tsps.
2	stalks	Green onions, cut finely	10	g.	2	stalks

<u>Sauce</u>

1. In a deep pan, brown the garlic in oil and set aside.

2. In the same pan, sauté the ground pork until oil comes out.

3. Stir in Mama Sita's Palabok Mix.

4. Gradually add 3 cups soup stock, stirring constantly until the sauce thickens.

5. Blanch noodles in soup stock. Drain and arrange on a platter.

6. Pour the sauce on top and garnish with toppings.

7. Serve with calamasi and fish sauce to taste.

BAKED TAHONG
(Spicy Baked Mussels)

Makes 4-6 servings.

			Metric	English
1	Kg.	Tahong (mussels), beards removed	1 Kg.	2.2 lbs.
1	pouch	Mama Sita's Caldereta Mix	50 g.	1 3/4 oz.
1/3	cup	Water	80 mL.	2 1/2 fl. oz.

1. Boil the mussels until they open.

2. Dissolve the Mama Sita's Caldereta (Spicy Sauce) Mix or Mama Sita's Barbecue Marinade Mix in 1/3 cup (80 ml.) of water.

3. Discard the half shell of the mussel which does not have meat.

4. Arrange mussels on a tray.

5. Brush the mussels with the mixture.

6. Bake at 350° F for 7-10 minutes or broil.

Mussels - without the calories of butter and cheese.

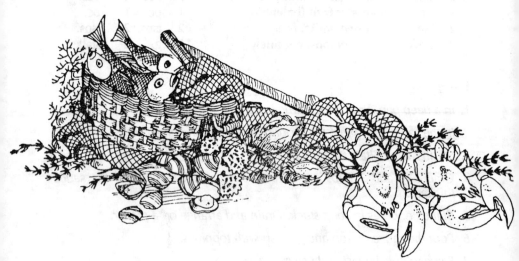

Chicken

"Filipinos living overseas can now savour 'genuine home food' through Mama Sita's sauces and mixes."

– Mary Ann Benitez
South China Morning Post
HongKong,
November 22, 1985

SOTANGHON SOUP
(Mung Bean Noodle Soup)

<u>Makes 6 servings.</u>

			Metric		English	
6	cups	Soup stock (see page 56)	1.5	li.	3	pints
1/4	Kg.	Chicken meat	1/4	Kg.	9	oz.
5	cloves	Garlic, crushed	15	g.	2	tsps
1	pc.	Onion, chopped	60	g.	2	oz.
1	pack	Sotanghon noodles (vermicelli), soaked in water for 30 minutes drained and set aside	100	g.	3 1/2	oz.
1	Tbsp.	Mama Sita's Spicy Sauce (Caldereta) Mix	1	Tbsp.	1	Tbsp.
1/4	cup	Dahon ng sibuyas (spring onions) cut into rings	10	g.		1/4 cup
5	cloves	Garlic, crushed	15	g.	2	tsps.
1	tsp.	Mama Sita's Annatto Powder (Achuete)	1	tsp.	1	tsp.
		Fish sauce (patis) to taste				

1 Fry garlic until golden brown. Set aside half.

2. In the same pan, sauté onion and chicken meat.

3. Add the soup stock and Mama Sita's Spicy Sauce (Caldereta) Mix. Let it boil.

4. Add the sotanghon noodles and cook for another 2 minutes.

5. Add Mama Sita's Annatto Powder (Achuete) and garnish with spring onion and fried garlic. Serve hot.

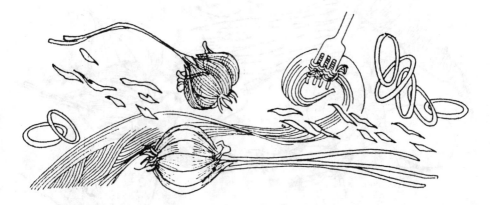

SINAMPALUKANG MANOK
(Chicken in Tamarind Broth)

Makes 4 servings.

			Metric		English	
1/2	Kg.	Chicken, cut into serving pieces	1/2	Kg.	17	oz.
1/2	Tali	Sitaw (long green beans)	100	g.	3 1/2	oz.
1	pc.	Tomato, sliced	40	g.	1 1/2	oz.
1	pc.	Onion, sliced	60	g.	2	oz.
2	Tbsps.	Mama Sita's Tamarind Seasoning Mix (Pang-Sinigang)	30	g.	2	Tbsps.
1	pc.	Sili (long green pepper)	10	g.	1	pc.
1	Tbsp.	Patis (fish sauce)	15	mL.	1	Tbsp.
2	Tbsps.	Cooking oil	30	mL.	2	Tbsps.
3	cups	Water	750	mL.	1 1/2	pint

1. Fry garlic in cooking oil. Add the onion, ginger and tomato.

2. Add the chicken, mix well. Season with fish sauce.

3. When the chicken is almost done, add water, bring to a boil.

4. Add Mama Sita's Tamarind Seasoning Mix, long green beans and long green pepper. Continue cooking until the vegetables are ready.

5. Serve with fish sauce.

CHICKEN LOLLIPOP

<u>*Makes 34 pieces.*</u>

			Metric		English	
1	Kg.	**Chicken wings**	1	Kg.	2.2	lbs.
1/3	cup	**Mama Sita's Caldereta** **(Spicy Sauce) Mix**	50	g.	1 1/2	oz.
1 2/3	cup	**All-purpose flour**	185	g.	7	oz.
1	cup	**Bread crumbs**	150	g.	5	oz.
4	cups	**Cooking oil**	1	liter	1	quart
2		**Eggs and salt to taste**	2		2	

1. Cut each wing on the joint and scrape off the meat to one end to form a lollipop.

2. Marinate in Mama Sita's Caldereta (Spicy Sauce) Mix for 30 minutes.

3. Dip in beaten eggs, dredge in flour and roll in breadcrumbs.

3. Deep fry over medium heat and drain over paper towels.

Variation : Marinate chicken in 1/4 cup Mama Sita's Barbecue Marinade overnight.

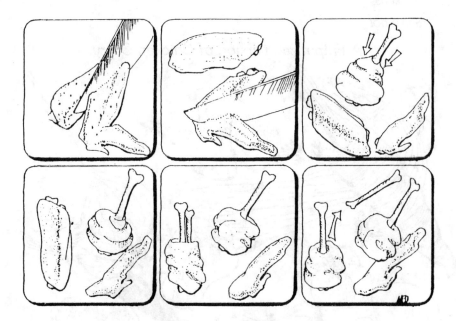

CHICKEN CURRY

Makes 8 servings.

			Metric		English	
1	Kg.	**Chicken, cut into serving pieces**	1	Kg.	2.2	lbs.
2	Tbsps.	**Cooking oil**	30	mL.	2	Tbsps.
4	cloves	**Garlic**	12	g.	1	tsp.
1	pc.	**Onion, sliced**	60	g.	2	oz.
1	pouch	**Mama Sita's Spicy Sauce (Caldereta) Mix dissolved in**	50	g.	1 3/4	oz.
1 1/2	cup	**Water**	360	mL.	12	fl.oz.
2	med. pcs.	**Bell pepper, cut into strips**	100	g.	3 1/2	oz.
1	cup	**Carrots, cubed**	200	g.	7	oz.
1/2	tsp.	**Curry powder**			1/2	tsp.
1	cup	**Potatoes, cubed and fried**	200	g	7	oz.
1	cup	**Thick coconut milk**	250	mL.	8	fl. oz.

1. *Sauté garlic and onion.*

2. *Add chicken, cook for 5 minutes.*

3. *Pour in Mama Sita's Spicy Sauce (Caldereta) Mix dissolved in water. Stir and bring to a boil.*

4. *Add carrots and potatoes. Simmer until vegetables are done.*

5. *Add bell pepper, coconut milk and curry powder. Simmer until the sauce thickens.*

   Serve hot.

A Filipinized version of Chicken Curry.

CHICKEN LIVER WITH MIXED VEGETABLES

Makes 4 servings

			Metric		English	
1/2 Kg.		Chicken liver, cut into halves, remove connective tissues and yellow spots	1/2 Kg.	1	lb.	
5	cloves	Garlic, crushed	15	g.	1	Tbsp.
1/2 cup		Onion, chopped	60	g.	2	oz.
5	Tbsps.	Mama Sita's Oyster Sauce	75	mL.	2 1/2	oz.
300	g.	Mixed vegetables (your choice of vegetables like sayote, Baguio beans, chicharo, cabbage, carrots, etc.)	300	g.	10	oz.
6	pcs.	Quail eggs, boiled and shelled	6	pcs.	6	pcs.
1	tsp.	Cornstarch, dissolved in	1	tsp.	1	tsp.
1/4 cup		Water	60	mL.	2	fl.oz.

1. Sauté garlic and onion.

2. Add liver and cook until medium rare (brown inside yet still bloody inside).

3. Stir in Mama Sita's Oyster Sauce. Simmer for 3 minutes.

4. Add the vegetables, one at a time, sayote first, Baguio beans and chicharo last. Stir fry.

5. Add the boiled eggs and cornstarch dissolved in water.

6. Cook until the sauce thickens.

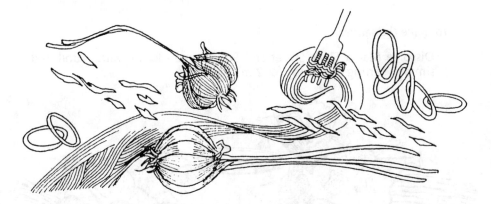

CHICKEN TWIST

<u>Makes 4-6 servings.</u>

			Metric		English	
1/2	Kg.	Boneless chicken breast, skinned	500	g.	17	oz.
1	cup	All-purpose flour	125	g.	4	oz.
2	pcs.	Eggs, beaten	2	pcs.	2	
1	cup	Breadcrumbs	150	g.	5	oz.
2	Tbsps.	Mama Sita's Caldereta Mix	20	g.	2	Tbsps.

<u>Dipping Sauce:</u>

1	pouch	Mama Sita's Sweet and Sour Sauce Mix	57	g.	2	oz.
3/4	cup	Water	180	mL.	6	fl. oz.

1. With the flat side of meat mallet or rolling pin, pound chicken lightly until 1/4" thick. Cut diagonally into strips, about 4 "x 1".

2. Sprinkle Mama Sita's Caldereta Mix and mix evenly over the meat. Marinate for about 30 minutes.

3. Dip each piece in flour, shake off excess.

4. Dip chicken in beaten egg, and roll in breadcrumbs.

5. Gently twist each strip several times. Chill chicken pieces for 30 minutes.

5. Heat cooking oil to 365° F. and fry chicken five pieces at a time until golden brown.

6. Drain well on paper towels.

7. Serve with Mama Sita's Sweet and Sour Sauce.

<u>To make the sauce:</u>

Dissolve Mama Sita's Sweet and Sour Sauce Mix in water. Boil and simmer, stirring constantly for 2 minutes.

FRIED CHICKEN WITH GINGER SAUCE

Makes 6 servings.

			Metric		English	
2	pcs.	Chicken breast, deboned and cut into serving pieces	1/2 Kg.		17	oz.
1/4	cup	Mama Sita's Barbecue Marinade	60	mL.	2	fl oz.
1	cup	Cooking oil	250	mL.	8	fl oz

Sauce :

			Metric		English	
1	Tbsp.	Cooking oil	15	mL.	1	Tbsp.
1/4	cup	Ginger root, preferably young ginger, strips	15	g.	1/4	cup
1/3	cup	Spring onions chopped	10	g.	1/3	cup
1	Tbsp.	Cooking oil	15	mL.	1	Tbsp.
1	Tbsp.	Cornstarch, dissolved in	15	g.	1	Tbsp.
1	cup	Water	240	mL.	8	fl oz.
2	Tbsps.	Mama Sita's Oyster Sauce	30	mL.	2	Tbsps.
1/4	tsp.	Sesame oil	1/4 tsp.		1/4	tsp.
1 1/2	tsp.	Rhum	1 1/2 tsp.		1 1/2	tsp.

1. Marinate chicken in Mama Sita's Barbecue Marinade for one hour. Deep fry. Drain and arrange in a platter.

2. Prepare the sauce.

   2.1 Stir fry ginger root and spring onions in cooking oil.

   2.1 Add cornstarch dissolved in water.

   2.2 When the sauce starts to thicken, add Mama Sita's Oyster Sauce, sesame oil and rhum.

   2.3 Stir the sauce until it thickens.

3. Pour over fried chicken breasts. Serve hot.

PASTEL DE POLLO
(Stewed Chicken with Pastry Crust)

Makes 4-6 servings

			Metric		English	
1	Kg.	Chicken meat diced	1	Kg.	2.2	lbs.
1 1/2 cups		Mushrooms quartered (optional)	150	g.	5	oz.
1 1/4 cups		Potatoes, cut into cubes and fried	1/4	Kg.	1/2 lb.	
1 1/4 cups		Carrots, cut into cubes and fried	1/4	Kg.	1/2 lb.	
1/2 cup		Grated cheese	80	g.	3	oz.
1	cup	Cream (optional)	250	g.	8	oz.
1	cup	Sibuyas tagalog (shallots), finely chopped	150	g.	5	oz.
6	Tbsps.	Cooking oil	90	mL.	3	fl.oz.
1	pouch	Mama Sita's Caldereta (Spicy Sauce) Mix	50	g.	1 3/4 oz.	
1/4 cup		Water	60	mL.	2	fl.oz.

1. Fry potatoes and carrots.

2. In another pan, sauté shallots in cooking oil.

3. Add the chicken and stir fry until the edges turn brown.

4. Add Mama Sita's Caldereta Mix dissolved in water and cook until the chicken is tender.

5. Add potatoes, carrots, mushrooms and cheese.

6. Stir over low fire until the cheese has melted.

7. Turn off the heat and stir in the cream.

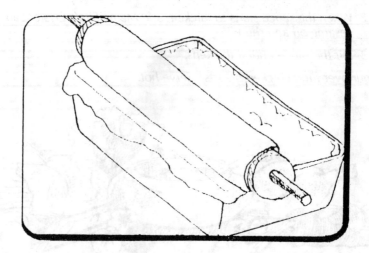

Pie Crust :

			Metric		English	
2 1/4 cup		Sifted all-purpose flour	247	g.	10	oz.
10	Tbsps.	Shortening	150	g.	5 1/4	oz.
1/4 tsp.		Salt	1/4	tsp.	1/4	tsp.
1/3 cup		Ice-cold water	80	mL.	2 1/2	fl.oz.
1		Eggyolk, beaten	1		1	

1. Sift flour and salt into a bowl.

2. With two knives or a pastry blender cut half of the shortening into the flour mixture until all the shortening has been well covered with flour. Then cut in the remaining half of shortening until the dough is sandy.

3. Sprinkle about 4 Tbsps water into the dough and gently blend it in. Add the rest of the water little by little as necessary.

4. Gather the dough into a ball and roll out the shape of your oven proof baking dish.

5. Roll out the dough.

To Assemble

1. Pour chicken mixture into an ovenproof dish.

2. Top with crust and pinch the edges to seal.

3. Prick the crust with a fork, brush with the beaten eggyolk and bake at 350° F until golden brown (about 15 minutes).

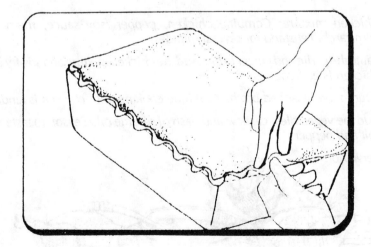

DICED CHICKEN WITH CASHEW NUTS

Makes 4 servings.

			Metric		English
2	Tbsps.	**Peanut oil or ordinary oil**	30 mL.	2	Tbsps.
2	tsps.	**Garlic, minced**	10 g.	2	tsps.
2	tsps.	**Ginger, minced**	10 g.	2	tsps.
1/2	cup	**Chicharo (snow peas)**	50 g.	1 3/4	oz.
1/2	cup	**Sweet peas**	85 g.	3	oz.
1/2	cup	**Toasted cashew, halves**	100 g.	3	oz.
	dash	**Sesame oil**			

Seasoned Broth:

1	cup	**Chicken broth**	250 mL.	8	fl. oz.
1	tsp.	**Sugar**	3 g.	1	tsp.
1 1/2	Tbsps.	**Mama Sita's Oyster Sauce**	20 mL.	1 1/2	Tbsps.
2	tsps.	**Cornstarch**	6 g.	2	tsps.

Chicken Mixture

1	cup	**Deboned chicken, diced**	100 g.	4	oz.
1	Tbsp.	**Soy sauce**	15 mL.	1	Tbsp.
1	Tbsp.	**Rhum**	15 mL.	1	Tbsp.
1	tsp.	**Cornstarch**	6 g.	1	tsp.
		Ground pepper to season			

1. _Chicken mixture: Combine chicken, pepper, soy sauce, rhum and cornstarch. Let stand for several minutes._

2. _Sauté the garlic and ginger in oil. Add the chicken mixture and stir-fry until chicken is half-cooked._

3. _Pour in the seasoned broth. Continue cooking until chicken is tender._

4. _Add the vegetables, cashew and dash of sesame oil. Season to taste with salt and pepper._

Serve hot.

ADOBO IN COCOSAUCE

Makes 4 servings.

		Metric		English	
1/2 Kg.	Chicken or pork, cut into serving pieces	1/2 Kg.		1	lb.
1 pouch	Mama Sita's Adobo Mix dissolved in	25	g	3 1/4	tsp.
1/4 cup	Water	60	mL.	2	fl.oz.
1/4 cup	Coconut milk	60	mL.	2	fl.oz.

1. In a casserole, combine the meat and the dissolved Mama Sita's Adobo Mix Cook over medium heat. When the sauce starts to boil, lower the heat and simmer.

2. When the meat is half-way cooked, add the coconut milk. Stir once in a while to prevent the sauce from sticking to the pan.

3. Continue cooking until the meat is tender and the sauce is slightly thick.

4. Remove from heat and serve with steamed rice.

CHICKEN AFRITADA
(Chicken Stewed with Potatoes
and Bell Peppers)

Makes 3 - 4 servings.

		Metric		English	
2 Tbsps.	Cooking oil	30	mL.	2	Tbsps.
1/2 Kg.	Chicken, cut into serving pieces	1/2 Kg.		1	lb.
1 pouch	Mama Sita's Menudo/Afritada Mix, dissolved in	30	g.	1	oz.
1 cup	Water	250	mL.	1	cup
1 cup	Potatoes, cubed, fried	190	g.	7	oz.
2 pieces	Red and green bell pepper, cut into strips	60	g.	2	oz.
1/2 cup	Green peas (optional)	90	g.	3	oz.

1. Stir fry chicken until golden brown.

2. Pour dissolved Mama Sita's Menudo/Afritada Mix, simmer until tender. Add hot water if necessary.

3. Add fried potatoes, bell pepper and green peas.

4. Simmer for 2 minutes.

CALDERETA
(Spicy Stew)

Makes 10 servings.

			Metric		English	
2	Tbsps.	Cooking oil	15	mL.	1	fl. oz.
1	cup	Potatoes, cubed	140	g.	5	oz.
1	Kg.	Chicken, cut into serving pieces	1	Kg.	2	lbs.
1	cup	Water	250	mL.	8	oz.
1	pouch	Mama Sita's Caldereta (Spicy Sauce) Mix	50	g.	2	oz.
1	pc.	Red bell pepper, cut into strips	40	g.	1 1/2	oz.
1/2	cup	Green peas	80	g.	3	oz.

1. Fry potato cubes in cooking oil. Remove potatoes and set aside.

2. Fry chicken until slightly brown on both sides. Add water, boil and simmer until tender.

3. Add Mama Sita's Caldereta Mix, potatoes and red bell pepper, cook until the vegetables are tender. Stir once in a while.

4. Just before removing from heat, add the green peas.

Note: Beef brisket (punta y pecho) may be used instead of chicken.

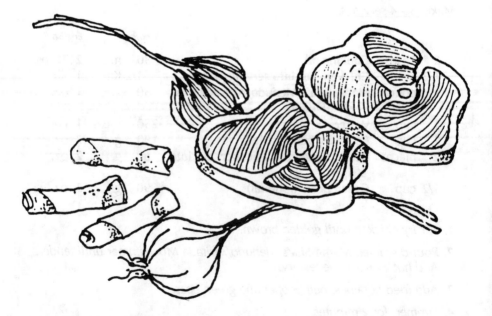

Meats

"The Kare-kare definitely evokes a great deal of response – either you love it or dislike it passionately."

– Evelyn Marie Joseph
The Star, Kuala Lumpur
July 14, 1986

ALMONDIGAS

Makes 6 servings.

			Metric		English	
1/2	Kg.	Ground beef	1/2 Kg.		17	oz.
1/2	cup	Singkamas(jicama)	100	g.	3 1/2	oz.
2	pcs.	Eggs, slightly beaten	2	pcs.	2	pcs.
1	pouch	Mama Sita's Barbecue Marinade Mix	50	g.	1 3/4	oz.
1	pc.	Onion, finely chopped	50	g.	1 3/4	oz.
1	stalk	Celery, finely chopped	20	g	1/4	cup
1/4	cup	Carrots , finely chopped	40	g.	1/2	oz.
1/2	cup	Cornstarch	40	g.	1 1/2	oz.
5	cups	Water	1 1/4 Li.		1/2	pint
1/4	cup	Onion, chopped	50	g.	1 3/4	oz.
2	cloves	Garlic, crushed	6	g.	1	tsp.
1	pack	Misua (wheat noodles)	120	g.	4	oz.
1	Tbsp.	Dahon ng sibuyas (spring onions)	20	g.	1	Tbsp.

1. Combine first 8 ingredients in a bowl and form into small balls of about 1/4 inch or 2 1/2 cm. in diameter.

2. Sauté garlic and onion.

3. Add water and bring to a boil.

4. Drop the meatballs one by one.

5. When meatballs are cooked, add misua and immediately remove from fire. Serve hot.

It is so satisfying it can be served as a main dish.

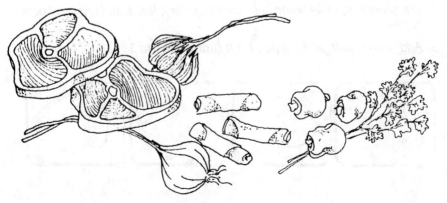

WONTON SOUP

Makes 6 servings

Ingredients for soup stock:

			Metric		English	
1/2 Kg.		Pork bones	1/2 Kg.		17	oz.
1/4 cup		Cooking oil	60	mL.	2	fl. oz.
1	pc.	Onion, quartered	60	g.	2	oz.
1	pc.	Carrot, diced	100	g.	3	oz.
1	pc.	Celery	100	g.	3	oz.
1	stalk	Leek	100	g.	3	oz.
8	cups	Water	2	li.	2	quarts
1	Tbsp.	Salt	15	g.	1	Tbsp.
1/4	tsp.	Pepper	1/4	tsp.	1/4	tsp.

Ingredients for Wonton Filling :

			Metric		English	
125	g.	Shrimps, shelled, deveined and chopped	125	g.	4	oz.
125	g.	Ground pork	125	g.	4	oz.
2	pcs.	Spring onions, chopped	10	g.	1	Tbsp.
2	Tbsps.	Mama Sita's Oyster Sauce	30	mL.	2	Tbsps.
1/4	tsp.	Garlic, chopped	1/4	tsp.	1/4	tsp.
1/4	tsp.	Ginger, chopped	1/4	tsp.	1/4	tsp.
30	pcs.	Wonton wrapper	30	pcs.	30	pcs.
1	pc.	Egg, beaten	1	pc.	1	pc

Soup Stock

1. Brown pork bones (either bake it in a 350 deg. F. oven for 10 - 15 minutes or fry it in cooking oil). Set aside.

2. In a saucepan, sauté onion, add carrots, celery, leeks, and browned pork bones.

3. Add water, salt and pepper. Let it simmer for 2 to 3 hours.

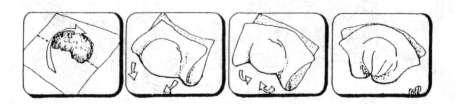

Wonton soup

1. In a bowl, combine ground pork, spring onions, Mama Sita's Oyster Sauce, garlic and ginger.

2. Scoop 1 teaspoon of the mixture on each square of wonton wrapper. Moisten the edge, fold diagonally over the filling to make a triangle and press the edge together to seal. Moisten the two corners at the back of the triangle and join them together.

3. Measure 7 cups (1.8 li.) of soup stock into a saucepan and let boil.

4. Drop the dumplings, five-six at a time and cook for 5 minutes. Set aside. (Do not overload in pan to avoid clinging together. Repeat until the dumplings are cooked.)

5. Bring soup stock to a boil and add fresh egg. Stir.

6. Drop the cooked dumplings and bring to a boil once more.

7. Sprinkle with spring onion and pepper.   Serve hot.

BEEF SINIGANG

Makes 4-6 servings.

			Metric		English	
6	cups	Water	1.5	Li.	1 1/2	quart
1	med.	Onion, peeled and quartered	100	g.	3 1/2	oz
1	large	Tomato, sliced into 1-inch Wedges	100	g.	3 1/2	oz
1	6"	Radish, peeled and cut into 1/4" diagonal slices	200	g.	7	oz.
1	cup	String beans, cut into 2" strips	100	g.	3 1/2	fl.oz.
2	pieces	Green chili pepper	20	g.	2	pcs.
4-5	Tbsps.	Mama Sita's Biglang Sinigang	60	g.	2	oz.
2 1/2	cups	Stewing beef, preferably bee brisket, bone-in or beef short ribs, cut into cubes (pork, fish shrimp, or scallops can also be used)	1/2	Kg.	17	oz.
1	cup	Green leafy vegetables (like Kangkong, spinach or mustard greens)	50	g.	2	oz.
1/2	tsp.	Patis (fish sauce)	1/2	tsp.	1/2	tsp.

1. Boil beef until tender, leaving about 4 cups broth.

2. Add Mama Sita's Biglang Sinigang and stir until well blended.

3. Add onion, tomatoes and radish. Let boil until vegetables are almost done.

4. Add leafy vegetables, long beans and pepper last.

5. Add patis.

SIOPAO ASADO
(Steamed Buns)

Filling:

			Metric		English	
1	Kg.	Pork kasim, thinly sliced	1	Kg.	2.2	lbs.
1	cup	Water	250	mL.	8	fl oz.
1/2 cup		Mama Sita's Barbecue Marinade	125	mL.	4	fl oz.
2	Tbsps.	Rhum	2	Tbsps.	2	Tbsps.
1	pc.	Bay leaf	1	pc.	1	pc.
2	Tbsps.	Sugar	2	Tbsps.	2	Tbsps.
1	Tbsp.	Cornstarch dissolved in	1	Tbsp.	1	Tbsp.
3	Tbsps.	Water	45	mL.	3	Tbsps.

Dough:

			Metric		English	
1 1/2	Tbsp.	Active yeast	1 1/2	Tbsp.	1 1/2	Tbsp.
2	cups	Lukewarm water	500	mL.	1	pint
1/2	cup	Sugar	125	g.	4	oz
6	cups	All-purpose flour	900	g.	2	lbs
1	Tbsp.	Baking soda	15	g.	1	Tbsp.
1	tsp.	Salt	5	g.	1	tsp.
1/2	cup	Shortening	125	g.	4	oz.
12	pcs.	Wax paper cut into 3" x 3" or 8 cm x 8 cm	12	pcs.	12	pcs.

Filling:

1. In a sauce pan combine the pork, water, Mama Sita's Barbecue Marinade, rum, sugar and bayleaf. Bring to a boil.

2. Lower the heat and simmer until the pork is tender.

3. Remove the meat and slice thinly.

4. Thicken the sauce with the cornstarch and water mixture.

5. Pour the sauce over the meat. Reserve.

Dough:

1. Dissolve yeast in lukewarm water.

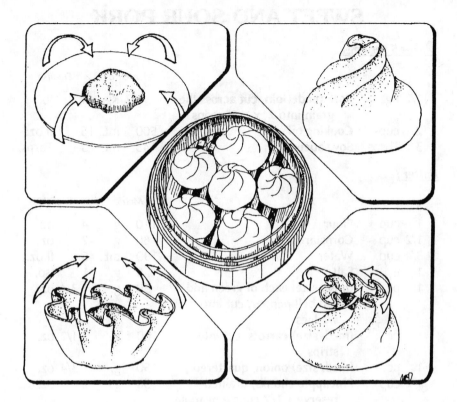

2. Add 1 tsp. sugar and let stand until bubbles form on the surface.

3. Add the rest of the ingredients.

4. Knead until smooth and elastic. Oil the surface, cover and let stand until it doubles its bulk.

5. Divide the dough into 12 equal-sized pieces. Flatten each piece into a 4 inch round, using floured hands to prevent the dough from sticking.

6. Place a tablespoon of filling onto the center of each round. Draw edges up and round filling; pinch and slightly twist to a point to seal.

7. Place 12 filled buns lined with wax paper, pointed side-up, in prepared steamer.

8. Steam covered for 10 to 15 minutes.

9. Remove from steamer, keep warm and serve immediately.

SWEET AND SOUR PORK

Makes 5 servings.

			Metric		Engflish	
1/2 Kg.		Pork tenderloin, cut across the grain into 2" x 1/2" strips	1/2	Kg. 1.1		lb.
2	cups	Cooking oil	500	mL. 16		fl.oz.
3	Tbsps.	Soy sauce	45	mL. 3		Tbsps.

Batter :

			Metric		English	
1	cup	Flour	110	g.	4	oz.
1/2	cup	Cornstarch	80	g.	2	oz.
3/4	cup	Water	190	mL.	6	fl.oz.
1	tsp.	Salt	5	g.	1	tsp.
1	pc.	(med. size) each of green and red bell pepper, cut into wedges	50	g.	1 3/4	oz.
1	pc.	(med. size) carrots, cut into strips	100	g.	3 1/2	oz.
1	pc.	(med. size) onion, quartered	50	g.	1 3/4	oz.
1/2	cup	Pineapple chunks, drained reserve 1 1/2 cups pineapple juice and dilute with	50	g.	2	oz.
1/2	cup	Water	125	mL.	4	fl.oz.
1	pouch	Mama Sita's Sweet and Sour Sauce Mix	57	g.	2	oz.

1. Marinate pork in soy sauce.

2. Combine flour, cornstarch, salt and water. Mix well to form a thin paste. Add pork and coat evenly with batter.

3. Heat oil over medium heat. Deep fry pork until golden brown. Place in a strainer to drain excess oil.

4. Place pork in a saucepan, combine vegetables, pineapple juice, pineapple chunks, and Mama Sita's Sweet and Sour Sauce Mix. Bring to a slow boil while stirring constantly until sauce thickens. Place pork in platter. Pour sauce over.

NAIIBA'NG LUMPIA
(Vietnamese Spring Rolls)

			Metric		English	
1	pack	Sotanghon (bean thread noodles) soaked, blanched and cut into 3 inch (10 cm.) lengths	100	g.	3 1/2	oz.
2	tsps.	Tenga'ng daga (dried tree ear mushrooms), soaked and coarsely chopped	2	tsps.	2	tsps.
1/2	pc.	Singkamas (jicama) chopped	50	g.	2	oz.
5	cloves	Garlic	1	tsp.	1	tsps.
1	pc.	Onion	80	g.	3	oz.
1	Tbsp.	Mama Sita's Oyster Sauce	15	mL.	1	Tbsp.
1	pouch	Mama Sita's Barbecue Marinade Mix	57	g.	2	oz.
3	pcs.	Eggs	3	pcs.	3	pcs.
1/2	Kg.	Ground Pork	1/2	Kg.	17	oz.
15	pcs.	Lumpia wrappers (spring roll wrappers) Cooking oil for deep frying	15	pcs.	15	pcs.

1. Combine first nine ingredients in a bowl and mix thoroughly.

2. Spoon two tablespoonfuls on each lumpia wrapper, roll and seal.

3. Deep fry and drain.

   Serve with dipping sauce.

Dipping Sauce

			Metric	English
2	Tbsp.	Grated carrots	20 g.	2 Tbsp.
1	Tbsp.	Grated radish	10 g.	1 Tbsp.
2	Tbsp.	Calamansi juice	30 mL.	2 Tbsp.
2	Tbsp.	Sugar	2 Tbsp.	2 Tbsp.
1/4	cup	Patis (fish sauce)	60 mL.	2 fl.oz.
1/4	cup	Suka (vinegar)	60 mL.	2 fl. oz.
5	cloves	Garlic, crushed.	1 Tbsp.	1 Tbsp.

Combine all ingredients and stir.

BEEF OR PORK WITH SPINACH

Makes 4 servings.

			Metric		English	
1/4	Kg.	Lomo (tenderloin, cut into thin strips)	1/4	Kg.	1/2	lb.
1	Tbsp.	Mama Sita's Barbecue Marinade	15	mL.	1	Tbsp.
2	Tbsps.	Cooking oil	30	mL.	2	Tbsps.
1/4	cup	Onion, chopped	40	g.	1	oz.
1/4	cup	Water	60	mL.	2	fl. oz.
1	bundle	Spinach or tong-choy (kangkong)	100	g.	4	oz.
1/4	tsp.	Pepper	1/4	tsp.	1/4	tsp.
2	Tbsps.	Cornstarch, dissolve in				
1/4	cup	Water	60	mL.	4	fl.oz
		Salt to taste				

1. Marinate meat in Mama sita's Barbecue Marinade for at least 30 minutes.

2. Heat oil in frying pan, sauté onion and meat until slightly brown.

3. Add water and spinach. Let boil. Stir and season with pepper.

4. Pour dissolved cornstarch. Stir until sauce thickens.

PORK ASADO

Makes 8 servings.

			Metric		English	
1	Kg	Whole lean pork	1	Kg.	2.2	lbs.
1	cup	Water	250	mL.	8	fl. oz.
1/2	cup	Mama Sita's Barbecue Marinade	125	mL.	4	fl. oz.
2	Tbsps.	Rhum	2	Tbsps.	2	Tbsps.
2	Tbsps.	Sugar	2	Tbsps.	2	Tbsps.
1	Tbsp.	Cornstarch dissolved in	1	Tbsp.	1	Tbsp.
3	Tbsps.	Water	45	mL.	3	Tbsps.

1. Combine the pork, water, Mama Sita's Barbecue Marinade, rhum, sugar and bayleaf. Bring to a boil.

2. Lower the heat and simmer until the pork is tender.

3. Remove the meat and slice thinly.

4. Thicken the sauce with the cornstarch and water mixture.

5. Pour the sauce over the meat.

PINSEC FRITO
(Crispy Wontons)

<u>*Makes 6-8 servings.*</u>

			Metric		English	
1/4	Kg.	**Ground pork**	1/4	Kg.	9	oz.
2 1/2	Tbsps.	**Dahon ng sibuyas (spring onion), finely chopped**	30	g.	2 1/2	Tbsps.
1	pc.	**Egg, beaten**	1	pc.	1	pc.
3	Tbsps.	**All-purpose flour**	23	g.	3	Tbsps.
1	Tbsp	**Cornstarch**	10	g.	1	Tbsp.
2	tsps.	**Mama Sita's Savory Sauce (Adobo) Mix**	10	g.	2	tsps.
1	Tbsp.	**Mama Sita's Oyster Sauce**	15	mL.	1	Tbsp.
50	pcs.	**Siomai wrapper**	50	pcs.	50	pcs.
2	cups	**Cooking oil, for deep frying**	1/2	li.	1	pint
1	pouch	**Mama Sita's Sweet and Sour Sauce Mix**	57	g.	2	oz.

1. *Combine ground pork, onion leaves, egg, flour, cornstarch, Mama Sita's Adobo Mix and Oyster Sauce. Mix thoroughly.*

2. *Scoop one teaspoon of the mixture onto each wrapper and fold two corners opposite each other and then the two others to seal like a pouch.*

3. *Deep fry over low flame until light brown. Place in a paper towel or strainer to drain excess oil.*

4. *Serve with Mama Sita's Sweet and Sour Sauce.*

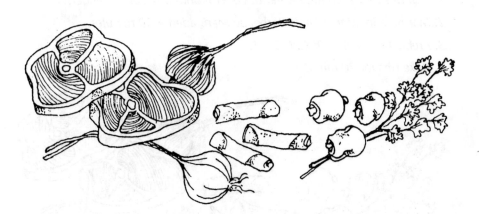

TOCINO
(Sweet Pork)

Makes 4 servings

		Metric	English
500 g	Pork shoulder (kasim)	1/2 Kg.	1.1 lb.
1 pouch	Mama Sita's Marinating (Tocino) Mix	75 g.	2.6 oz.

1. *Slice meat 1/4" thick.*

2. *Sprinkle Mama Sita's Marinating (Tocino) Mix evenly over meat and knead until juice of meat comes out.*

3. *When ready to cook, preheat a charcoal or gas-fired grill.*

4. *Broil meat one side at a time or cook with 1/2-3/4 cup water in wok. Simmer until the water dries up and fry in its own fat.*

BAKED SPARE RIBS

Makes 6 servings.

		Metric	English
1 Kg.	Meaty Spare ribs	1 Kg.	2.2 lbs.
1/2 cup	Mama Sita's Barbecue Marinade	125 mL.	4 fl.oz.

1. *Boil ribs in just enough water to cover it until it becomes tender.*

2. *Marinate in Mama Sita's Barbecue Marinade for 30 minutes.*

3. *Preheat oven at 180° C. (350° F.).*

4. *Bake ribs for 20 minutes.*

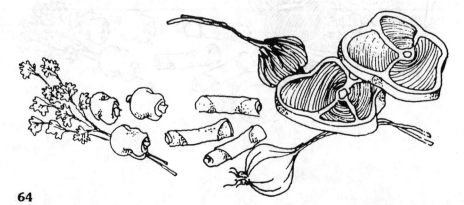

DINUGUAN
(Blood Stew)

<u>*Makes 4 servings.*</u>

			Metric		English	
1/2	Kg	Paypay ng baka (beef chuck)	1/2	Kg.	17	oz.
1 1/2	cup	Beef blood	375	mL.	12	fl. oz.
2	Tbsps.	Mama Sita's Tamarind Mix	25	g.	2	Tbsps.
		dissolved in				
1	cup	Water	250	mL.	8	fl. oz.
1/2	pc.	Onion, chopped	40	g.	1/3	cup
3	cloves	Garlic, crushed	12	g.	2	tsps.
1	piece	Long green pepper	15	g.	1	pc.
1	tsp.	Salt	5	g.	1	tsp.
2	Tbsps.	Cooking oil	30	mL.	2	Tbsps.
1	cup	Water, to boil beef	250	mL.	8	fl. oz.
		(add more water if necessary)				
		Patis (fish sauce) to taste				

1. *Boil the beef with salt until tender. Set aside.*

2. *In a saucepan, sauté garlic and onion.*

3. *Add the boiled meat and stir-fry for 5 minutes.*

4. *Gradually add the blood while stirring constantly and bring to a boil. (If not in liquid form be sure to cut the blood into small pieces before adding to the meat.)*

5. *Add the Mama Sita's Tamarind Mix dissolved in water .*

6. *Season with patis and cook covered five minutes more.*

7. *Add the long green pepper just before removing from the fire. Keep covered and serve hot with puto or steamed rice.*

With this recipe you will never have to worry about the raw taste of vinegar.

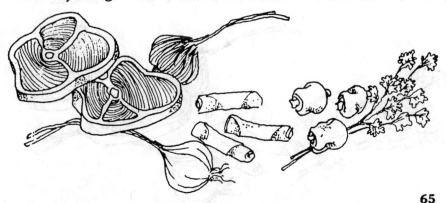

BOLA-BOLA CON SALZA AGRIO-DULCE
(Meat Balls with Sweet & Sour Sauce)

<u>Makes 4-6 servings.</u>

			Metric		English	
1	pc.	Carrot, chopped	60	g.	2	oz..
1	pc.	Celery, chopped	30	g.	1	oz..
1/2	Kg	Ground beef	1/2	Kg.	1	lbs.
2	pcs.	Eggs	2	pcs.	2	pcs.
2	tsps.	Salt	2	tsps.	2	tsps.
1	tsp.	Freshly ground blackpepper	1	tsp.	1	tsp.
2	cups	Cooking oil	500	mL.	1	pint
4	cloves	Garlic, crushed	12	g.	2	tsps.
1	piece	Onion, chopped	50	g.	1 1/2	oz.
1	piece	Red bell pepper, sliced	50	g.	1 1/2	oz
1	pouch	Mama Sita's Sweet and Sour Sauce Mix dissolved in	57	g	2	oz.
1/2	cup	Water	120	mL.	4	fl. oz.
1/4	cup	Flour	30	g.	1	oz.
1	cup	Water	250	mL.	8	fl. oz.

1. Combine ground beef, celery, carrots, onion and Mama Sita's Barbecue Marinade and mix thoroughly. Chill for about 30 minutes.

2. Form into meatballs.

3. Roll the meatballs in flour.

4. Heat the cooking oil and fry the meatballs.

5. Sauté garlic and onions, add the Mama Sita's Sweet and Sour Sauce Mix.

6. Gradually pour in the water.

7. Bring to a boil while stirring constantly and simmer until thick.

8. Add meatballs and bell pepper and simmer for another 5 minutes.

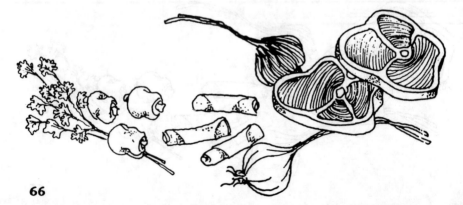

LUMPIANG SHANGHAI
(Spring Rolls)

Makes 45 pieces. Good for 6-8 servings.

			English		**Metric**	
1/4	Kg.	**Ground pork**	1/4	Kg.	9	oz.
1/3	cup	**Finely chopped jicama (singkamas)**	40	g.	1	oz.
2	Tbsps.	**Finely chopped carrots**	30	g.	1	oz.
1	pc.	**Onion, finely chopped**	60	g.	2	oz.
1	Tbsp.	**Mama Sita's Barbecue Marinade Mix**	10	g.	1	Tbsp.
1	whole	**Egg, beaten**	1		1	
1	tsp.	**Sesame oil**	1	tsp.	1	tsp.
1/2	tsp.	**Salt**	1/2	tsp.	1	tsp.
2	Tbsps.	**Cornstarch**	20	g.	2	Tbsps.
2	Tbsps.	**Cornstarch (mixed with one egg)**	20	g.	2	Tbsps.
15	pcs.	**Spring roll (lumpia) wrappers**	15	pcs.	15	pcs.
		Cooking oil for deep frying				

1. Combine first 9 ingredients in a bowl.

2. Spoon 1 Tbsp. of the mixture on the lumpia wrapper. Roll and seal by brushing the edge with the cornstarch-egg mixture. Repeat process until you have used up the filling.

3. Deep fry in preheated 350° F oil until golden brown, about 8-10 minutes. Drain off excess oil. Cut into three pieces.

4. Serve with Mama Sita's Sweet and Sour Sauce.

Variation : Use 1 tbsp. Mama Sita's Caldereta Mix in place of Mama Sita's Barbecue Marinade Mix

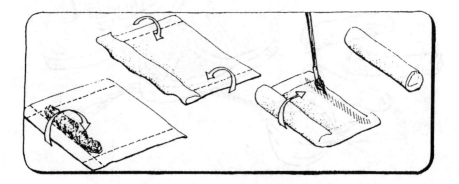

LECHON KAWALI
(Crispy Pork)

<u>*Makes 6 servings.*</u>

			Metric		English	
1	Kg.	**Pork liempo (side bacon with rind)**	1	Kg.	2.2	lbs.
4	cups	**Water**	1	li.	1	quart
		Salt to taste				
4	cups	**Cooking oil**	1	li.	1	quart
		Mama Sita's (Sarsa Ng Lechon)				
		All Purpose Sauce				

1. *Combine pork, water and salt in a saucepan and bring to a boil.*

2. *Lower the heat and simmer until the pork is tender. Drain the pork and cool. Reserve the stock for some other purpose.*

3. *Prick skin with fork and rub with rock salt.*

4. *Heat cooking oil in a deep fryer or wok at high heat. Fry pork until golden brown and crispy. Cut into serving pieces and serve with Mama Sita's All Purpose Sauce (Sarsa Ng Lechon), pickled papaya (achara) and rice.*

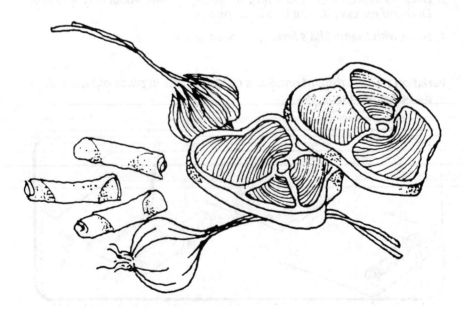

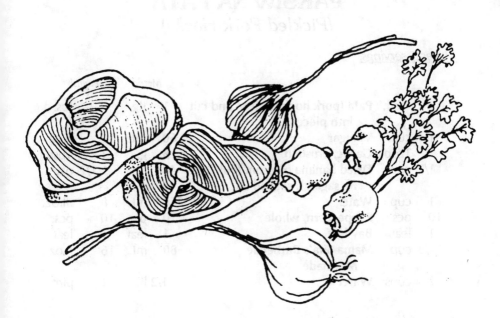

PAKSIW NA LECHON
(Pork Stewed in Tangy Liver Sauce)

<u>Makes 8 servings.</u>

			Metric		English	
1	Kg.	Roast pork (lechon), cut into serving pieces	1	Kg.	2.2	lbs.
1	Tbsp.	Garlic, chopped	15	g.	1	Tbsp.
1/2	cup	Onion, chopped	60	g.	2	oz.
1	pc.	Bayleaf	1	pc.	1	pc.
3	bottles	Mama Sita's (Sarsa ng Lechon) All Purpose Sauce	936	g.	1	quart
2	Tbsps.	Vinegar	30	mL.	2	Tbsps.
8	pcs.	Whole peppercorn	1	tsp.	1	tsp.
1/2	cup	Water	120	mL.	4	fl.oz.
1	tsp.	Salt				

1. Combine all ingredients in a saucepan and cover. Boil.

2. Stir and simmer for about half an hour over low heat.

3. Remove the bayleaf and serve with rice.

PAKSIW NA PATA
(Pickled Pork Hocks)

Makes 5 servings.

			Metric		English	
1	med.	Pata (pork hocks), clean and cut into pieces	1	Kg.	2.2	lbs.
1/4	cup	Vinegar	60	mL.	2	fl.oz.
1	Tbsp.	Garlic, crushed	15	g.	1	Tbsp.
1/2	cup	Dried banana blossom (bulaklak ng saging), soaked in	40	g.	1 1/2	oz.
1	cup	Water	250	mL.	8	fl.oz.
10	pcs.	Peppercorn, whole	10	pcs.	10	pcs.
1	leaf	Bay leaf	1	leaf	1	leaf
1/3	cup	Mama Sita's Barbecue Marinade	80	mL.	16	fl.oz
2	cups	Water	1/2 li.		1	pint

1. Combine all ingredients.

2. Boil, then simmer for one hour or longer until tender. Stir once in a while to prevent from sticking.

BARBECUE

Makes about 20 sticks barbecue.

			Metric		English	
1	Kg.	Kasim (pork shoulder), cut into 2"x1"x1/4" strips. (Sirloin steak, lamb, shrimp, scallops, calamari or fish fillet can also be used)	1	Kg.	2	lbs.
1/2	cup	Mama Sita's Barbecue Marinade	120	mL.	4	fl. oz.

1. In a bowl, combine pieces of meat and Mama Sita's Barbecue Marinade.

2. Marinate for at least 3 hours.   If using shrimp, scallops, calamari or fish fillet, marinate just for 10 minutes. When ready to grill, skew meat with bamboo sticks.

3. Grill over live charcoal about 2-3 minutes on each side or to desired doneness.

4 Brush occasionally with the marinade mixed with cooking oil.

BEEF WITH SNOW PEAS

Makes 4 servings:

			Metric		English	
300	g.	Beef tenderloin or sirloin, sliced into thin bite-sized strips	300	g.	10	oz.
1	Tbsp.	Gin	15	mL.	1	Tbsp.
1 1/2 tsp.		Mama Sita's Barbecue Marinade	1 1/2 tsp.		1 1/2	tsp.
1	Tbsp.	Fresh ginger juice or dash of ginger powder	15	mL.	1	Tbsp.
1	Tbsp.	Cornstarch	10	g.	1	Tbsp.
100	g.	Chicharo (snow peas), stems and strings removed	100	g.	3	oz.
3	Tbsps.	Cooking oil	3	Tbsps.	3	Tbsp.
1	clove	Garlic, crushed	1 1/4 tsp.		1 1/4	tsp.
1 1/2 Tbsps.		Mama Sita's Barbecue Marinade	20	mL.		1/2 Tbsp.

1. Combine the first 5 ingredients and set aside.

2. Stir-fry snow peas quickly in 1 Tbsp. cooking oil for at least one minute. Set aside.

3. Sauté garlic and onion.

4. Add the beef and stir-fry.

5. Add Mama Sita's Barbecue Marinade and gin.

6. On a serving platter, make a nest out of the snow peas, spoon the beef in the middle.

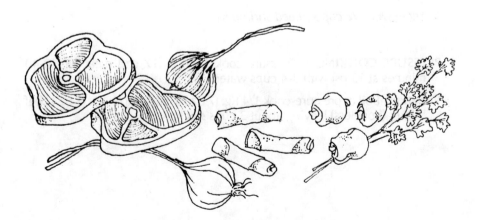

KARE-KARE
(Oxtail Stewed in a rich Peanut Sauce)

Makes 4 servings.

			Metric		English	
1/4 Kg.		Buntot ng baka (oxtail), cleaned and cut into serving pieces	1/4 Kg.		9	oz.
1/4 Kg.		Tuwalya ng baka (tripe), cleaned and cut into serving pieces	1/4 Kg.		9	oz.
2	med. pcs.	Eggplant, cut into 1" lengths	200	g.	7	oz.
5	strings	String beans (sitaw), cut into 1" slices	100	g.	3 1/2	oz.
1	small pc.	Banana heart, cut diagonally into 1/2"	250	g.	8	oz.
1	pouch	Mama Sita's Stew Base Mix (Pang Kare-kare) (just add 3/4 cup (190 g.) of peanut butter) or	50	g.	2	oz.
1	pouch	Mama Sita's Peanut Sauce Mix (Kare-kare) water to boil meat	57	g.	2	oz.
1	tsp.	Salt	1	tsp.	1	tsp.
1/2 cup		Sauteed shrimp fry (bagoong alamang)	50	g.	1 1/2	oz.

1. _Boil or pressure-cook oxtail and tripe with 1 tsp. salt until tender, leaving about 3 cups (750 ml.) stock._

2. _Add vegetables (banana heart first and long beans last) and simmer until half-cooked._

3. _Pour Mama Sita's Stew Base Mix and stir until well blended._

4. _Add peanut butter. Simmer for 2 minutes or until thick._

5. _Serve with 1/2 cup sauteed shrimp fry._

PRESSURE COOKING : Pressure-cook 1/2 Kg. (17 oz.) meat for 30-40 minutes at 15 psi with 3-4 cups water.

Variation : Boil or pressure-cook 1/4 Kg. (7 oz.) tripe and 1/4 Kg. (7 oz.) beef brisket (boneless) leaving about 3 cups stock.

BEEF WITH OYSTER SAUCE

Makes 4 servings.

			Metric		English	
1/4 Kg.		**Beef sirloin, pounded with the back of a knife and cut into strips**	1/4 Kg.		1/2 lb.	
1	Tbsp.	**Soy sauce**	15	mL.	1	Tbsp.
1	cup	**Chicharo (snow peas)**	100	g.	3	oz.
2	Tbsps.	**Cooking oil**	30	mL.	2	Tbsps.
5	cloves	**Garlic, crushed**	15	g.	1	Tbsp.
2	slices	**Ginger, minced**	10	g.	2	tsps.
1	pc.	**Onion, thinly sliced**	30	g.	1	oz.
2	Tbsps.	**Mama Sita's Oyster Sauce**	30	mL.	2	Tbsp.
1	tsp.	**Gin**	5	mL.	1	tsp.

1. Marinate beef in soy sauce for about 30 minutes.

2. Stir fry chicharo in 1 Tbsp. cooking oil for at least 1 minute. Remove the cooked chicharo from the pan and set aside.

3. In the same pan, sauté garlic in the remaining cooking oil until golden brown.

4. Add the ginger, stir-fry.

5. Add the onions and cook until transparent.

6. Add the beef and cook until slightly brown. Add the Mama Sita's Oyster Sauce and gin. If the mixture seems to be sticking to the bottom of the pan, add 2 tablespoons (30 ml.) water.

7. Add the reserved chicharo. Stir and serve hot.

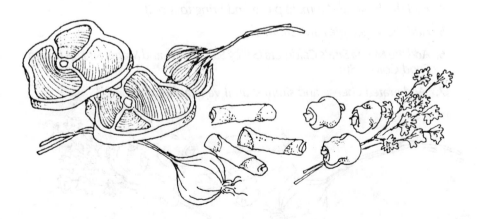

CALLOS

Makes 8 servings.

			Metric		English	
1	Kg.	Tuwalya ng baka (tripe) sliced into 2" lengths	1	Kg.	2.2	lbs.
1/4	Kg.	Buntot ng baka (oxtail), deboned and cut into 2" lengths	1/4	Kg.	9	oz.
3	Tbsps.	Cooking oil	45	mL.	3	Tbsps.
2	cloves	Garlic, crushed	5	g.	1	tsp.
1	pc.	Onion, minced	60	g.	2	oz.
1	can	Beef vienna sausage, cut 1/4" crosswise	226	g.	8	oz.
4	tsps.	Tomato paste	4	tsps.	4	tsps.
1	pouch	Mama Sita's Caldereta (Spicy Sauce) Mix	50	g.	1.7	oz.
1	pc.	Green bell pepper, diced	80	g.	2	oz.
1	can	Chickpeas	200	g.	8	oz.
2	pcs.	Potatoes, diced	100	g.	3	oz.
2	Tbsps.	Grated cheese	2	Tbsps.	2	Tbsps.
2	pcs.	Carrots, diced	100	g.	3	oz.
1	pc.	Chorizo de bilbao, sliced diagonally (optional)	1	pc.	1	pc.
2	tsps.	Mama Sita's Annatto Food Color dissolved in	2	tsps.	2	tsps.
1	Tbsp.	Water	1	Tbsp.	1	Tbsp.

1. Boil oxtail and tripe until tender, leaving about 3 cups broth.

2. Heat oil in sauce pot and sauté garlic and onion.

3. Add sausage, chorizo and meat. Stir.

4. Add the broth and tomato paste and bring to a boil.

5. Add the vegetables and simmer.

6. Add the Mama Sita's Caldereta (Spicy Sauce) Mix and Mama Sita's Annatto Food Color. Stir.

7. Add grated cheese and simmer until vegetables are done.

CHILI CON CARNE

Makes 6-8 servings.

			Metric		English	
1/2	cup	Red kidney beans	100	g.	3 1/2	oz.
2	Tbsps.	Cooking oil	30	g.	2	Tbsps.
1	bulb	Garlic, minced	20	g.	2	Tbsps.
1	piece	Onion, minced	50	g.	2 1/2	oz.
1	piece	Red bell pepper, chopped	50	g.	3	oz.
1	tsp.	Salt	2	g.	1	tsp.
1/2	Kg.	Ground beef	1/2 Kg.		17	oz.
1	can	Tomato paste	227	g.	8	oz.
1	pouch	Mama Sita's Caldereta (Spicy Sauce) Mix				
1 1/2	cup	Water	375	mL.	12	fl oz.

1. Soak the beans overnight and boil until tender. Set aside.

2. In a heavy skillet, sauté garlic, onion, bell pepper and salt.

3. Add the meat and cook until light brown and vegetables are tender.

4. Stir in remaining ingredients.

5. Cover and simmer for 10 minutes.

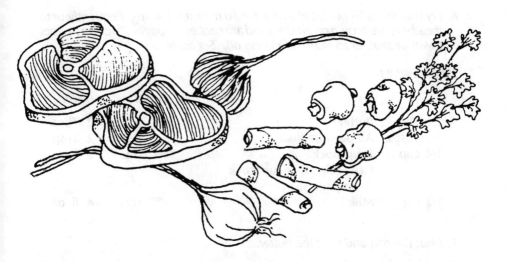

MEATBALLS IN WHITE SAUCE

			Metric		English	
2	slices	Loaf bread, chopped finely	2	slices	2	slices
1/2	cup	Milk	125	mL.	4	fl.oz.
1/4	Kg.	Ground pork	1/4	Kg.	9	oz.
1/4	Kg.	Ground beef	1/4	Kg.	9	oz.
2	pcs.	Eggs, slightly beaten	2	pcs.	2	pcs.
1/2	cup	Onion, chopped	80	g.	3	oz.
1	pouch	Mama Sita's Barbecue Marinade Mix	50	g.	1.7	oz.
1/8	tsp.	Iodized salt	1/8	tsp.	1/8	tsp.
5	pcs.	Dahon ng sibuyas (spring onions)	10	g.	2	Tbsp.
1	cup	Cooking oil	250	mL.	8	fl. oz.

1. Soak chopped bread in milk. Stir with a fork and let stand at room temperature for 5 minutes so that the bread can absorb the milk.

2. Combine the ground pork and beef in a large bowl.

3. Add the egg, onion, Mama Sita's Barbecue Marinade Mix, salt and spring onion.

4. Toss meat mixture with a fork until thoroughly combined.

5. Shape into round meatballs.

6. Fry meatballs 15 pieces at a time for 10 minutes, turning frequently until meatballs are brown on all sides and are cooked through. Place on a paper towel or strainer to drain off excess oil. Set aside.

White Sauce :

			Metric		English	
2	Tbsps.	Butter	30	g.	2	Tbsp.
2	Tbsps.	All-purpose flour	30	g.	2	Tbsp.
3/4	cup	Soup stock (see recipe for soup stock on page 56)	180	mL.	6	fl. oz.
1/2	cup	Milk	125	mL.	4	fl. oz.

1. Heat the pan and melt the butter.

2. Add the flour to the butter all at once and stir with a wooden spoon until smooth.

3. Gradually add soup stock, while stirring constantly.

4. Set the fire to medium heat and keep on stirring until it starts to boil.

5. Add the milk and lower the heat, and cook 3 minutes longer or until sauce is thick and smooth.

6. Add meatballs to the white sauce, toss gently to coat well. Remove from heat and serve.

MEATLOAF

Makes 8 servings.

			Metric		English	
1/2	Kg.	Ground beef	1/2	Kg.	1.1	lb.
1/2	Kg.	Ground pork	1/2	Kg.	1.1	lb.
3	slices	Bread finely chopped and soaked in	3	slices	3	slices
1/4	cup	Water	60	mL.	1/4	cup
3	pcs.	Egg, beaten	3	pcs.	3	pcs,
1	cup	Raisins	120	g.	4	oz.
1	pc.	Onion	60	g.	2	oz.
1	can	Vienna sausage, sliced into 4	145	g.	5	oz.
1	pouch	Mama Sita's Spicy Sauce (Caldereta) Mix	50	g.	1.7	oz.

1. Combine all ingredients and mix thoroughly.

2. Line bottom of 9" x 5" x 3" pan with wax paper.

3. Transfer mixed ingredients and bake at 350°F for one hour.

4. Drain excess fat and let cool before slicing.

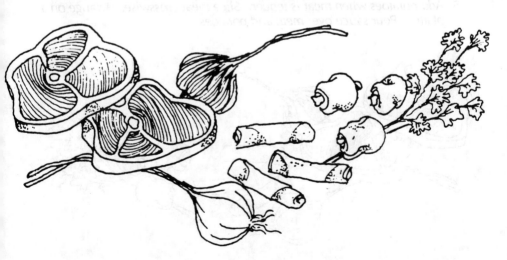

MECHADO
(Beef Braised in Savory Shallot Sauce)

<u>Makes 6-8 servings.</u>

			Metric		English	
1	cup	Pork fat, cut into strips	100	g.	7	oz.
1	Kg.	Kabilugan or Punta y Pecho (whole beef round or beef brisket	1	Kg.	2.2	lbs.
	1/2 cup	Cooking oil	125	mL.	4	fl. oz.
	6 1/2 cups	Shallots (sibuyas tagalog) or any other kind of onion, finely chopped	1	Kg.	2.2	lb.
1	pouch	Mama Sita's Adobo Mix, dissolved in	50	g.	1.7	oz.
1	cup	Water	250	mL.	8	fl. oz.
	1/2 tsp.	Mama Sita's Annatto Powder (Achuete)	1/2	tsp.	1	tsp.
2	pcs.	Potatoes, cut into cubes and fried	200	g.	7	oz.
		Salt to taste				

1. *Lard the beef by cutting through with thin knife and inserting fat strips.*

2. *Marinate beef in Mama Sita's Adobo Mix for at least 4 hours.*

3. *Sauté the shallots and set aside.*

4. *In the same oil, fry the beef until it is well browned. Add shallots, Mama Sita's Annatto Powder, marinade and salt. Cover and simmer. Add water if necessary. Reduce heat. Stir once in a while.*

5. *Add potatoes when meat is tender. Slice meat crosswise. Arrange on a platter. Pour sauce over meat and potatoes.*

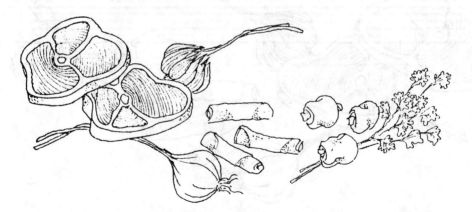

STUFFED MUSHROOM WITH OYSTER SAUCE

Makes 20-25 piece.

			Metric		English	
1	cup	**Ground pork**	1/4	Kg.	1/2	lb.
2	pcs.	**Onions, finely chopped**	40	g.	1	oz.
2	Tbsps.	**Flour**	30	g.	1	oz.
1	pc.	**Egg**	1	pc.	1	pc.
1/2	tsp.	**White pepper**	1/2	tsp.	1/2	tsp.
2	tsps.	**Sesame oil**	10	mL.	2	tsps.
1/2	tsp.	**Salt**	1/2	tsp.	1/2	tsp.
20-25	pcs.	**Small dried mushrooms**	65	g.	2	oz.
1	Tbsp.	**Mama Sita's Oyster Sauce**	15	mL.	1	Tbsp.

1. Soak mushrooms in plain water overnight. Cut the stems and drain.

2. Mix the first seven ingredients thoroughly.

3. Stuff mushroom with the mixture.

4. Arrange in a steamer and steam for at least 1 hour or until meat is tender.

5. Serve with Mama Sita's Oyster Sauce on top.

LONGGANISA
(Breakfast Sausage)

			Metric		English	
1/2	Kg	**Ground pork**	1/2	Kg.	17	oz.
1	pouch	**Mama Sita's Marinating (Tocino) Mix**	75	g.	2 2/3	oz.
5	cloves	**Garlic, crushed and chopped**	15	g.	3	tsp.
1/4	tsp.	**Blackpepper**	1/4	tsp.	1/4	tsp.
1/8	tsp.	**Salt**	1/8	tsp.	1/8	tsp.

1. Combine all ingredients in a bowl. Mix thoroughly. Let stand in the refrigerator for at least two hours.

2. Roll two tablespoons of the mixture in waxed paper.

3. Remove from wax paper and fry in hot oil until brown.

4. Serve hot.

Note: This can be stored in the freezer. Thaw before frying.

"A dynasty of five generations of queens of Filipino Gastronomy live today in Manila and have become the ambassadors of Filipino cooking to the world.

The Marigold Commodities Corporation sell Mama Sita's instant food mixes and sauces which go into the pot to capture at once the authentic filipino taste in your dishes."

— Margaret Chan
Wine & Dine — Singapore
August/September 1989

MAMA SITA'S PRODUCTS

Annatto Powder *Achuete*	10 g.	1/3	oz.
Barbecue Marinade Mix	50 g.	1.7	oz.
Marinating Mix *Tocino*	75 g.	2.6	oz.
Marinating Mix *Tocino*	100 g.	3.5	oz.
Meat Stew Mix *Menudo/Afritada*	30 g.	1.0	oz.
Peanut Sauce Mix *kare-Kare*	57 g.	2.0	oz.
Peanut Sauce Mix *Kare-Kare*	100 g.	3.5	oz.
Savory Sauce Mix *Adobo*	25 g.	7/8	oz.
Savory Sauce Mix *Adobo*	50 g.	1.7	oz.
Shrimp Gravy Mix *Palabok*	57 g.	2.0	oz.
Spicy Sauce Mix *Caldereta*	50 g.	1.7	oz.
Stew Base Mix *Pang Kare-Kare*	50 g.	1.7	oz.
Stir Fry Mix *Pancit Canton/Chopsuey*	40 g.	1.4	oz.
Sweet and Sour Mix	57 g.	2.0	oz.
Tamarind Seasoning Mix *Sinigang*	25 g.	7/8	oz.
Tamarind Seasoning Mix *Sinigang*	50 g.	1.7	oz.
Barbecue Marinade	150 mL.	5	fl.oz.
Barbecue Marinade	350 mL.	11.8	fl.oz.
Oyster Sauce	150 mL.	5	fl.oz.
Oyster Sauce	350 mL.	11.8	fl.oz.
Oyster Sauce	680 mL.	23	fl.oz.
Premium Vinegar	355 mL.	12	fl.oz.
Sauce for Roasts – Reg. *Sarsa ng Lechon*	300 mL.	11	oz.
Sauce for Roasts – Hot *Sarsa ng Lechon*	300 mL.	11	oz.
Tamarind Paste *Biglang Sinigang*	240 mL.	8	oz.

> *"Riding on the crest of the instant and the natural craze, Mama Sita became a by-word of quality..."*
>
> – Richie Benavides
> Ang Pahayagang Malaya, Manila
> August 12, 1985

INDEX

CHICKEN

Adobo in Coco Sauce   53

Caldereta (Spicy Stew)   54

Chicken Afritada (Chicken   53
Stewed with Potatoes and Bell Peppers)

Chicken Curry   46

Chicken Liver with Mixed Vegetables   47

Chicken Lollipop   45

Chicken Twist   48

Diced Chicken with Cashew Nuts   52

Fried Chicken with Ginger Sauce   49

Pastel Del Pollo   50
(Stewed Chicken with Pastry Crust)

Sinampalukang Manok
(Tamarind Flavored Chicken Soup)   44

Sotanghon Soup
(Mung Bean noodle Soup)   43

MEAT

Almondigas   55

Baked Spare Ribs   64

Barbecue   70

Beef or Pork with Spinach   62

Beef Sinigang   57

Beef with Oyster Sauce   73

Beef with Snow Peas   71

Bola-Bola Con Salza Agrio-Dulce   66
(Meatballs with Sweet and Sour Sauce)

Callos   74

Chili Con Carne   75

Dinuguan (Blood Stew)   65

Kare-Kare
(Oxtail Stewed in a Rich Peanut Sauce)   72

Lechon Kawali (Crispy Pork)   68

Longganisa (Breakfast Sausage)   79

Lumpiang Shanghai (Spring Rolls)   67

Meatballs in White Sauce   76

Meatloaf   77

Mechado   78

Naiiba'ng Lumpia
(Vietnamese Spring Rolls)   61

Paksiw na Lechon
(Pork Stewed in a Tangy Liver Sauce)   69

Paksiw na Pata (Pickled-in Pork Hocks) 70

Pinsec Frito (Crispy Wontons)   63

Pork Asado 62

Stuffed Mushroom with Oyster Sauce   79

Sweet and Sour Pork   60

Tocino (Sweet Pork)   64

Wonton Soup   56

SEAFOODS

Adobong Pusit (Squid Adobo)   32

Baked Tahong (Spicy Baked Mussels)   42

Calamares (Squid Rings)   36

Crab Lumpia (Crab Rolls) 35

Easy Shrimps   40

Garlic Squid   33

Guinataang Hipon   40
(Shrimps in Coconut Sauce)

Paella Pilipina   26

Pinangat sa Gata
(Fish Poached in Coconut Sauce)   34

Rellenong Bangus 29

Saucy Clams   28

Seafood Chowder   23

Sinigang na Hipon 22

Special Pancit Palabok   41
(Noodles with Shrimp Gravy)

Spicy Sizzling Shrimps   33

Steamed Lapu-Lapu   37

Stuffed Squid   30

Sweet and Sour Fish   28

Tocino'ng Isda   34

Tom Yum Goong   21

Tuna Empanada   24

VEGETABLES

Adobong Kangkong   1

Arroz Ala Mama Sita   2

Chopsuey   4

Creamy Adobo Dip   9

Fried Bean Curd with Oyster Sauce   19

Fried Rice with Oyster Sauce   16

Ginisang Munggo (Sauteed Mung Beans)   18

Ginisang Togue (Sauteed Bean Sprouts)   12

Kangkong with Oyster Sauce   3

Lumpiang Gulay (Vegetable Rolls)   8

Mama Sita's Lettuce Salad   15

Pancit Bihon Guisado   11
(Stir Fried Vegetables over Rice Noodles)

Pancit Buko with Oyster Sauce   5

Pechay Flowers   17

Pinakbet (Tropical Vegetable Stew)   6

Sotanghon Bihon Guisado   14
(Stir Fried noodles)

Spicy Sitaw   7

Stir Fried Vegetbles with Garlic Sauce   10

Ukoy (Shrimp Vegetable Fritters)   13

Vegetable Soup   1

Vegetables Unlimited   3

LIST OF RETAIL OUTLETS IN KEY CITIES
WORLDWIDE

ABU DHABI. U. A. E.

Ayda International
P.O. Box 6743
Abu Dhabi, U. A. E.

AGANA, GUAM

Great Mart Enterprises
P. O. Box G. A. Agana
Guam 96910
Tel Nos. 646-5736
        646-5743

ALKHOBAR, K.S.A.

Saudi Arabia Oriental Food Company
P.O. Box 1020
Alkhobar 31952 K.S.A.
Tel. No. (03) 894-9314/895-2684

Al Humillase Trading Est.

P.O. Box 3146
Alkhibar, K. S. A.
Tel. No. 895-2157/2810

AMMAN, JORDAN

Safeway International
P. O. Box 96065
Amman, Jordan

AMSTERDAM, NETHERLANDS

Chung Hing Hong
Chinees Toko
Oude Zijds Voorburgwal 37-39
1012 EJ Amsterdam - C
Tel No. (020) 258-233

ANTWERP,BELGIUM

Sun Wah Supermarket
Van Wesenbeke Straat
2000 Antwerp
Tel No. 03-2333142

ATHENS, GREECE

M & D Kastanas O.E. Philippine Products
Distomou 58, Agia Barbara, Egaleo
Athens, Greece 12351
Tel. No. 544-0491

BAHRAIN, U. A. E.

Midway Supermarket
P. O. Box 643, Bahrain
U. A. E.
Tel. No. 253100/320384/663594

BERGEN, NORWAY

Sidhu Continental Food Store
Roga gaten 19
5000 Bergen, Norway

BERN, SWITZERLAND

Eve's Asien - Shop
Goten Strasse 4
3018 Bumpliz
Tel No. (031) 55-03-07

BONN, GERMANY

Holland Shop Oriental Foods
Wurzerstrasse 116
Bonn Bad Godesberg Germany
Ruf 352-796

BRUNEI DARUSSALAAM

Hua Ho Dept. Store & Supermarket
Hanimatul Saadiah Lot 1991
Jalan Godong 3180
Brunei Darussalaam

CHICAGO, ILL. U.S.A.

Global Marketing Corp.
3229 So. Shields
Chicago Illinois 60616
Tel. No. (312) 2256445

COPENHAGEN, DENMARK

Premacell
Vesterbrogade 86, 1620
Copenhagen V Denmark

DAMMAM, K.S.A.

Shaflout Est.
P. O. Box 1711
Dammam 31441, K. S. A.
Tel. No. (03) 833-4391/832-6752

DUBAI, U. A. E.

Safeway Emirates
P.O. Box 6664
Dubai, U. A. E.

DUSSELDORF, GERMANY

Asiatische Lebensmittel
Lindenstrasse 99
4000 Dusseldorf 1
Tel. No. 0211/685714

GARAPAN, SAIPAN

Wendell's Shoppers Mart
Garapan, Saipan MP 96950
Tel. No. (670) 234-9515 / 234-1610

GENEVA, SWITZERLAND

Bambou Shop
Bd James - Fazy 8
1201 Geneva, Switzerland
Tel. No. 022/31 93 33

GENT, BELGIUM

Makati Supermarket
Zuistation Straat 7
9000 Gent
Tel No. (091) 23-97-13

JONA, SWITZERLAND

Far East Trade & Travel Services
St. Gallerstrasse 166
CH - 8645 Jona
Switzerland

HAMBURG, GERMANY

Batavia Shop
Hofweg 46
2000 Hamburg 76
Germany
Tel. No. 042-2 29-97-44

HONG KONG

Silver Creation
Shop 132-133, 1st Floor
World-Wide Plaza Central
Hong Kong
Tel. No. 5-222727

JEDDAH, K. S. A.

Saudi Oasis Est.
Jeddah, K. S. A.
Tel. No. (02) 651-7096/5276

JERSEY CITY, N.J. U. S. A.

Phil-Am Food Mart
685 Newark Ave.
Jersey City N.J. U.S.A. 07306
Tel. No. (201) 963-0461/420-8595

JUBAIL, K. S. A.

Hassan Ali Al Thuwaimir
P. O. Box 134, Jubail
K. S. A. 31951

KATIKATI, NEW ZEALAND

Victoria's Sari Sari Store
504 Lockington Rd.,
Kati Kati, New Zealand

KOBE, JAPAN

Hayashi Shoten
1-3-19 Sakae Machi
Chuo-ku Kobe, Japan
Tel. No. (078) 321-2764

LONDON, ENGLAND

Matahari Impex (Fax East) Ltd.
11-12 Hogarth Place, Earls Court
London SW5
Tel. No. 071-370-1041

LOS ANGELES, CALIFORNIA U.S.A.

99 Ranch Market # 4
988 N. Hill St. #101
L.A. Ca. 90012

MADRID, SPAIN

Casa Extremo Oriente
Galeria Subterranea Parking
Plaza de España
Tel. No. 2421464-28013

NAGOYA, JAPAN

Sun lemon
5-9-34 Sake Naka-ku
Nagoya, Japan
Tel. No. (052) 241-4700

ONTARIO, CANADA

Pilipino Five-0 Ltd.
1198 The Queens Way
Etobicok, Ontario
Canada M8Z 1R6
Tel. No. (416) 251-2009

OSAKA, JAPAN

Goka Shoten
Exceed Nihon-bashi,
1F 2-15-10
Nihon Bashi Chuo-ku
Japan
Tel. No. (06) 646-0547

PORT MORESBY, PAPUA NEW GUINEA

Taurama Self-Service Supermarket
P. O. Box 1180, Port Moresby
Tel. No. 251991 / 251111

RIYADH, K.S.A.

Al Amro Shopping Center
P. O. Box 9695, Riyadh 11423
Tel. No. (01) 465-9987 / 491-2358

Panda Distribution Center
P.O. Box 21650
Riyadh, K.S.A.

ROME, ITALY

Ditta Castroni
Via Ottaviano, 55
Roma, Italy
Tel. No. 351474

SAFAT, KUWAIT

Al Mohammed Tifoni Co.
P.O. Box 4361
Safat 13044 Kuwait
Tel. No. 481-2980

SAN FRANCISCCO, CA. U.S.A.

Philippine Grocery
4929 Mission St.
SF, CA U.S.A.
Tel. No. (415) 584-4465

SEATTLE, WA. U. S. A.

Beacon Market
2500 Beacon Ave., So.
Seattle, Wa. 98144
Tel. No. (206) 328-9202; 323-2050

Uwajimaya
P. O. Box 3003, Seattle
Washington 98114
Tel. No. (206) 624-6248

TOKYO, JAPAN

J.C. Foods
Ameyoko Center Building
4-7-8 Ueno Taito-ku
Tokyo, Japan
Tel. No. (03) 3834-6666

VIENNA, AUSTRIA

Orient Shop
Nashmarkt 973
1040 Vienna, Austria
Tel No. 587-8730

VIRGINIA BEACH, VA. U.S.A.

Oriental Express Groceries
Parkway Shopping Center
1512 Lynnhaven Parkway
Virginia Beach, VA 23456
Office Tel. No. (808) 471-7237

WILMINGTON, DEL. U.S.A.

Asia Food Market
2110 Kirkwood Highway
Wilmington, Del. U.S.A. 19805
Tel. No. (302) 633-0488

WOODSIDE, N.Y. U.S.A.

Phil-Am Foodmart
40-03 70th St.
Woodside, N.Y. U.S.A.

YOKOHAMA, JAPAN

Eisho Food
187 Yamashit-cho
Naka-ku Yokohama
Tel. No. (045) 641-1576

For free cooking demonstrations and inquiries, write or call:

Mama Sita's Sauces & Mixes
131 F. Manalo St. San Juan
Metro Manila, Philippines
Tel. Nos. 70-94-17 & 70-94-35
Fax No. (632) 780369